What People Are Saying About This Book

"Very funny, with more than one kernel of truth hidden in the satire...if you've ever thought there was one part of your body you'd like to change, you'll get good belly laughs from this book. Ironically, although *Big Girls' Guide* is a self-help parody, Bunkie's message ... being happy with ourselves ... is the most important self-help of all. And if laughter truly is the best medicine, you'll definitely be healthier after reading this book!"
—Darel Snodgrass, Morning Arts & Music Host,
WKNO-FM, Memphis

"*The Big Girls' Guide to Life* celebrates living large and does it with sass, heart and swift wit. Lynn provides hilarious tips for robust-sized living, and she doesn't wince, even when addressing Granny panties (don't) and seat width (be rich and fly first class). She tackles touchy issues—unkindness, relationships, parties—and invokes the sexy spirits of non-Twiggy icons like Queen Latifah and Marilyn Monroe. Brazen and fun, a much-needed larger-than-life toast to the Junoesque sisterhood!"
—Lori Hall Steele, Contributor, *Detroit Free Press*
& Associate Editor, *Traverse.*

"Growing up and living life as a Big Girl in our society with its 'thin is in' mentality is no easy task . . . Bunkie tells it like it is or how it should be for 'large-boned gals' as she outlines basic guidelines for food, exercise, and other essentials. This tongue-in-cheek expository will lift your spirits and tickle your funny bone ... Bunkie's flaming hot sarcasm will have you rolling with laughter ... share it with your girlfriends, they'll thank you for it!"
— Elyse Thibodeaux, *The Beaumont Examiner*

"Put on your best Sunday hats; it's time for the most potent form of networking—women's social club talk. Reading Bunkie Lynn is akin to that low chatter that happens after the chicken salad sandwiches are memories, iced tea has turned Long Island and shades are drawn against the afternoon sun. Loosen up your girdles, girls, Bunkie reveals all the secrets with the wit and grace of a Southerner. *The Big Girls' Guide to Life* is a hilarious retort to today's health and fashion trends. Meeting adjourned, ladies, let's have a pastry!"

—Kim Conner, columnist, *Carolina PageTurner*

"I was devastated to reach the end, I could not easily put it down. **Big Girls' Guide** is pure genius! Passionate, poignant and uplifting with a dump-truck load of humor. This book works on all sorts of levels for all sorts of people, whether you're a 'Big Girl with Attitude' or not. Bunkie's words are hilarious and filled with hope!"

—Katrina Neylon, CEO, ***Van Kleeck & Gardner***

The Big Girls' Guide to Life

A Plus-Sized Jaunt
Through A Body-Obsessed World

Bunkie Lynn

LadyBug
Publishing LLC
Hendersonville, TN

Contributions by C.J. Bach

LadyBug Publishing, LLC

Publisher Cataloging-in-Publication Data

Lynn, Bunkie.
The big girls' guide to life : a plus-sized jaunt through
a body-obsessed world / Bunkie Lynn. — Hendersonville, Tenn. :
LadyBug Publishing, 2004

p. ; cm.
ISBN: 0-9721301-1-X

1. Body image in women—Humor. 2. Self-acceptance.
3. Self-esteem in women. 4. Overweight women—Humor.
5. Overweight women—Psychology. 6. Beauty, Personal—Humor.
7. Body size—Psychological aspects. I. Title.

BF697.5.B63 L96 2004   2003111185
158/.1/082—dc22   CIP

Cover by K. Kimmey Design, Loudon, Tennessee

Illustrations by Rick Baldwin, Knoxville, Tennessee

Visit the author's Web site at www.bunkielynn.com
for event and appearance information

Trademark Usage

In this book, I use specific product brand names because it sounds so much better to say, "I need a sackful of Krystals®, right now," versus, "I sure could use two or three pounds of those little square, steamed hamburgers with mustard and pickle, each individually wrapped and placed in a large white paper bag." To clarify, I'm not the official or unofficial spokesperson for anything named herein. I'm just a Big Girl sharing my preferences strictly to entertain the public. Readers of this book, as well as the owners of the brand names, should take no offense, and should be advised that I have no association with either the brand names or the companies that produce the goods. And now to give credit where credit is due:

Contents

Acknowledgments

I am indebted to the following people for their assistance, friendship, support, and guidance in my life: Carol and Tim; Klair and Richard; Nancy; Teresa; my editor, Mary Jo Zazueta; Katrina; author Cameron Michaels; Shannon and Jimmy; Beverly; Rob; Jan; my Texas girlfriends Amy, Mollye, Kelleyelle, Deb, Sherrie, Anne, Kathy, Lori, Denise, Mary, Jenna, Debbie, Vicki and Robin; my sister and brother; my son and lively Labs; my husband, Mike, who is the Absolute Best Husband in the History of the Universe; and my parents, for the sometimes torturous, often hysterically funny and always loving family in which I was raised. Thanks for accepting me no matter what size or shape I may be.

STOP: Read This Right Now!

This book is the product of my overactive imagination in a purely satirical effort to make people laugh. If you're unable to make the distinction between reality and satire, and let's face it, we all get confused sometimes, let me assist: the lifestyle "advice" in this book is not intended to be taken seriously in any way, shape, or manner. I am not a doctor nor do I play one on TV. I'm no health expert. This is not a self-help book! I'm just a Big Girl who writes humor and diet fanatics should not adhere to any actions or behaviors described in these pages as if they were steps on the path towards improved health.

The events, places, and characters in this book are purely fictitious; their resemblance to anything or anybody, living or dead, is coincidental, unintentional, and has been incorrectly inferred by the reader. No liabilities will be assumed regarding the misinterpretation of the contents, in whole or in part, as fact.

This work is dedicated to Big Girls everywhere who constantly struggle with their weight and food issues, and who often feel that today's body-obsessed society is overwhelmingly against them. This book is by no means promoting an unhealthy lifestyle; I know the value of being fit, eating right, and obtaining the benefits of exercise. However, as an over-forty Big Girl who has battled a weight problem my entire life, I have at long last learned that happiness is not strictly about size. We must each possess self-esteem in order to live joyfully, experience happiness, and maintain balance. I hope this book will help you laugh in the face of adversity, examine your priorities and your lifestyle, and then seek the pleasure that may be right under your nose, or your jelly doughnut. Good luck on your journey, wherever it may take you.

To Big Girls of the World ... Salute!

You could,
if you really wanted to.

—Ted Weber

Author's Note

I remember dress shopping with my mother when I was about six years old. Shopping is not a regular activity when you're on a tight budget, but we always bought new school clothes and a new Easter outfit. At this particular Easter shopping venture, I remember my mother rifling through the dress racks in frustration while I watched my brother sleep in his stroller. My mom inquired as to the location of the girl's size 6X dresses. I distinctly remember that the clerk, a rude woman wearing an ugly print shift, looked me up and down and then said sarcastically, "Mmmm … she'll need every inch of a 6X, won't she? We don't have a 'chubby' department. You might try another store." My mom smiled at me and I pretended that I wasn't crushed.

This routine happened over and over as I continued to gain weight and as the semi-annual ritual of clothes shopping marched on. My embarrassment wasn't just limited to clothes, either. I was blessed with very large, flat feet. I'll never forget the shoe clerk who, after searching the entire stockroom for several pairs of youthful-looking shoes in a woman's size 7, declared, "This child's foot is very large … will you need paddles? She could just wear the boxes."

By the age of eleven I was somewhat of a tomboy, because it seemed easier to be a tomboy and wear blue jeans than to face Pure-D Shopping Hell where none of the cute clothes were made in my size. At this point, I was probably about thirty pounds overweight. I remember my parents placed me on an early version of a high-protein diet at our doctor's stern advice ... I could eat veggies, no carbohydrates, and Fresca®. I drank so much Fresca I thought I would turn light green. To this day, I *hate* Fresca.

All those nice, colorful Diet and Nutrition pamphlets from the doctor were useless. I probably lost a few pounds here and there, but at night I'd sneak into the kitchen and gobble Oreos® out of the cookie jar. In junior high, I was so miserable I ate my entire lunch during the mid-morning break. I sat at a table by myself, cramming chips and a still-frozen tuna fish sandwich into my mouth. I took comfort from this bizarre ritual. During the actual lunch break, I fished in my coin purse to scrape together enough money to buy a hot meal from the school cafeteria, or chips and a Coke®. I loved hot school lunches ... warm yeast rolls, mashed potatoes and gravy. I even ate the vegetables ... it felt so good going down.

My parents were confounded as to how I continued to gain weight when they tried to maintain strict control over my eating. And therein lies part of the problem. Their method of dealing with my weight was to become ever stricter. We'd sit down and have a heart-to-heart chat, usually with tears and an incredible amount of guilt on my part, and then my parents would declare the terms.

"If you don't lose five pounds this week, there will be no more piano lessons." And then when I began to cry, they would say, "You have such a pretty face. Don't you understand why this is so important?" Oh, I understood, all right. I understood anger and frustration at the fact that my parents gave me an ultimatum—but no tools to achieve the prize. There were rarely fruits or vegetables at our house. My mom is a great cook and her specialties included spaghetti, lots of garlic bread, sloppy joes and chips, hamburgers on the grill ... things my brother and sister and parents ate in healthy doses, but I ate in excess. There were always bowls of ice cream or homemade cookies for dessert, and when we needed comfort, my mom offered pie with her advice.

I know I'm responsible for my own actions, but there I sat, expected to avoid eating what was on the table and still lose weight. Gee, here's a hard question … Would I rather have a piece of my mom's cake or an apple? There aren't any apples in the house, so I'll take the cake, please, Alex, for ten pounds!

I was told to exercise and lose weight, but I had no road map. I didn't really want to lose weight, I loved food. As an asthmatic, I hated gym with a passion, and I would rather have taken a beating than exercise in the humidity of our southeast Texas neighborhood. The harder my parents pushed, the more stubbornly I resisted.

Friday mornings often featured a hellish parade into the bathroom. I mournfully led my parents into the Torture Chamber and they watched me get onto the scale, to review my week's weight loss and issue the verdict. "Well, that's it! No more piano lessons. And next week, if you don't lose five pounds, you'll be grounded."

I was grounded a lot. I missed football games and lost all my privileges. Try explaining to your friends that you're grounded because you are fat … not an easy thing to do, so I lied about it. I still didn't lose weight. Finally my parents gave up because my seriously ill grandmother moved in with us, and with an elderly woman and three rambunctious kids to care for, I think they simply became too stressed out to deal with me, particularly as I didn't show the slightest inclination to follow their orders. Even my grandmother, whom I loved dearly, would accost me in the hallway and say, "You sure would make your parents happy if you lost weight."

What would make *me* happy? Food sure did. Deep down I knew my family had my best interests at heart. I knew they loved me, and I knew I should lose weight. But there was no desire to do so, zero positive motivation. So I continued to eat what I wanted and instead became the comic of my class, the jokester who could deflect any comment about my size or appearance.

In high school I was probably about forty pounds overweight, but because I was a good student with a great sense of humor, I made close friends who are still loyal to me to this day. I was blessed with the gift of a sarcastic wit, and I kept everybody laughing on a daily basis. As to fashion, it was the era of overalls, painter pants, and tee shirts, so despite the fact that I wasn't teen model material, I was able to participate in a few trends and soon developed my own style.

My senior year in high school was one of the happiest periods in my life. I was the editor of the school newspaper and my regular, humorous column about life as a misfit was responsible for my selection as the Wittiest Girl in the class. I belonged to the German club, the French club, the Journalism club, and the You-Name-It club, just to get out of the house and avoid the discussion of my weight. I had friends out the ying-yang. I had a key role in the school musical, playing the part of the fat, evil queen, of course, but I knocked 'em dead. And I had a *boyfriend!* Someone to talk with, someone who was smart and funny … and we went to the prom! Me, *the Big Girl,* went to the prom! I even lost weight for the event, and then promptly gained it all back, but those photos sure looked great. I later learned my boyfriend was gay. Oh, well. It was fun while it lasted. *Gotcha,* world! My weight didn't prevent me from having fun and going to my *senior prom!*

College was truly liberating for me … two hundred and

fifty miles away from home and prying eyes, and the dorm cafeteria food was amazing. Three hot meals a day plus unlimited trips to the Coke machine and midnight pizza deliveries. To deflect my parents' questions about my eating habits, in my junior year I surprised them by earning a coveted slot as a dorm resident assistant with free room and board. My parents were so stunned, and relieved at the waiver of half my college expenses, they never said another word about my weight. I graduated with a degree in filmmaking and twenty more pounds on my frame. My parents are proud of me, I know, but the issue of my heaviness always hovered over us, as it still does today. I can run out the door in any kind of clothing six days a week and feel relatively comfortable, but it takes me three hours to decide what to wear to my parents' house, trying to find that one outfit that will accentuate my "pretty face" and hide my *problem.*

To this day my family and certain friends feel obligated to inform me about the latest diet that works like a charm, or give me the most wonderful book on nutrition from the Mayo Clinic. This obligation also takes the form of Christmas presents, like the electric fat-free indoor grill, complete with LOW-FAT RECIPES! Now, who'd like some eggnog and pie?

I was fortunate to meet and marry a man who loves me for who I am. Although he's never said one word about my weight, I'm sure he'd be thrilled if I could maintain a weight loss, because he knows that I might like myself more. He endures my endless attempts at this diet or that diet, and we even trained together and walked in a half-marathon, where I'm proud to say I won my medal, dammit, as a Big Girl. Of course, he and some friends pulled my fat ass up some killer hills and I was nearly comatose at the finish line, but I did it, and I hope to do it again, once my toenails grow back.

I miraculously sustained a healthy pregnancy while sixty pounds overweight. I proudly declared to everyone that I only gained twenty-five pounds! My pregnancy was truly the one time in my life when I was motivated to eat healthy and maintain self-control. But once my son was delivered, I returned to my old habits, and here I remain.

I'm now in my mid-forties ... after a lifetime of being overweight, the knee joints are shot and I'm on blood pressure medicine. The ten pounds I could drop in a week in my twenties now take over a month to come off, at great effort. Why is it that my brain, which I know for a fact contains a goodly amount of intelligence, can't overcome incessant urges to eat? Why is it that despite my knowledge of the horrors of obesity, despite the highs of exercise, I just can't refuse that brownie?

I keep trying. As my shuffling weight registers up and down on my personal collection of bathroom scales, and as I devour diet books and health advice with a vengeance, yet take little permanent action, I have learned to like myself a little more each day. I think middle age does something to a person ... you finally reach the point where you realize that your hours are numbered, and that if you have to spend one more day bowing and scraping to please others, you're wasting precious time.

Most overweight people have a dream or a goal: If I could just wear a size *(fill in the blank)*, I'd be happy. If I could just lose *(fill in the blank)* pounds, I'd be happy. I'm here to tell you, as so many others have told us before, *it ain't gonna happen*. A number on a scale isn't what happiness is necessarily about. Sure, we'd look better and our health would no doubt be improved, but then what? Big Girls often use food as an emotional crutch and we carry that crutch with us day and night, everywhere we go.

Until we learn to let go of our emotional ties to food, we could lose a hundred pounds on a "magic" diet and still not find the happiness we think is out there for us. A noted on-air therapist said to a woman who was contemplating gastric bypass surgery that the only component in her overweight lifestyle she could control through surgery was the size of her stomach. Until she learned to deal with the real issues behind her food addiction, nothing would help her unlock her heart and find contentment. Experts say this is true of any addictive behavior, and eating is an addiction for most folks with a weight issue. We crave the comfort that our addiction brings us, when, in fact, it's killing us.

The best example I know about the sorrows of addiction is the story of a former employer of mine. This man was a true genius. He was brilliant, an excellent salesman, and a super storyteller. He was also a very scary alcoholic, verbally and mentally abusive to those around him. Once, in a rare moment of honesty, he openly admitted to us the pain his addiction caused him, the pain we could all feel for him but never dared discuss. My colleagues and I intervened and packed him off to a well-known clinic for treatment. He came home dry as a bone, but meaner than a snake. He scared the bejeezus out of me, and through my attendance at Al-Anon meetings, I learned that alcohol was the balm that soothed his demons. Without that balm, he couldn't control his anger or his emotions. He lived in sober turmoil for as long as he could stand it, finally succumbing once more to excessive drink and tragically, suicide.

Like my former employer, I'm sometimes in pain. I'd love to be magically fit and trim, but I'm not so certain I'd know how to act, how to react to the world, how to truly let down my guard. I'm not sure I have the ability to comfort myself in any way other than through food. Food junkies joke that "at least we're not addicted to alcohol or pills," but in our hearts we know that food is a slow killer and we need a twelve-step program just like any other addict. We tell ourselves that if only we had a personal trainer and a personal chef, and a personal, big-ass padlock on the pantry and refrigerator, *then* we'd be in control. I once joked to my close friend, who is also a Big Girl, that there should be a Fat Camp for grown-ups, where Big Girls could be taken against their will and endure forced weight loss and trench digging in 100-degree heat. But once Fat Camp is over, *bam,* you've got to live with yourself again, and there's the real issue.

The general public doesn't perceive being overweight as a serious addiction, and I can understand why ... if *you* can drop ten pounds in a month to wear that new dress to your high school reunion, why can't *I* shed one hundred pounds? Isn't my problem just a question of weakness, really? Aren't I ashamed of myself? Don't I have any self-control?

Yes, I am ashamed sometimes, but I'm learning to deal with that. For the most part these days, I like my life. And no, truthfully, I don't have one ounce of self-control. Is there a pill for that?

Chapter One

Big Girls Defined

As a charter member of the exclusive Big Girls' Club, it is my sole responsibility to enlighten you and lay the wreath of charity, harmony, and clarity at your feet. Being a Big Girl isn't just about size, missy. You must possess some serious whoop-ass attitude to make it through life as a Big Girl. You must have crocodile-thick skin, a vein of sarcasm the size of the Amazon River, a stubborn streak that rivals Halley's comet, and the oh-so-important portfolio of rude gestures and verbal comebacks to accompany all of the above.

Here is the end all, be all, definitive meaning of Big Girl (*biggus girlus* for any nauseating, scholarly types who have earned multiple advanced degrees to instruct us on how not to be a Big Girl, as if they have a *clue* about what it's like to be one of us): *A Big Girl is someone, preferably of the female persuasion, who is Junoesque in stature, be it height or weight.*

Oh, please don't say you don't know who Juno was … did you fall asleep every day in World History or what? A Big Girl's positive attributes are not only physically enhanced, her heart is rather enlarged as well, and we're not just talking triple bypass here, but the fact that Big Girls want everybody to like us, so we grovel and put up with crap no reasonable person would endure, just to be your Close Friend. On the Mr. Hyde-

Whoop-Ass Attitude side of this issue, if you had to deal with so much Big Girl make-nice b.s. every day, when everyone else in this scum-sucking world is staring at you and judging you and offering you celery sticks, and you're trying to be the Best Friend to the winner of this year's Jerk-a-Thon, you'd have rather an attitude thing going on now, wouldn't you? Damn straight! Big Girls learn to fight back when we have to, and believe me, it can get ugly, *fast.*

You are most definitely *NOT* a Big Girl if you weigh less than one hundred and forty pounds dripping wet, unless you are three feet tall, and then, God bless you, there are other, more appropriate groups to which you should belong. Neither are you found in the elite Big Girl ranks if you top six feet in height and weigh about thirty pounds, because then, my dear, you are what we rather distastefully refer to as a *Supermodel* ... don't get me started, or I'll have to twist that big head of glossy hair right off your skinny neck and force-feed it triple cheese-burgers.

Wearing the Big Girl mantle means you can expertly avert any type of social crisis, including catcalls from lowlife construction workers, a split in the backside of your khakis, or the loss of a button from your blouse as it pops into your companion's soup. Big Girls are born knowing the proper way to flip a bird in the direction of an insult; how to waltz into an ice cream parlor alone and order a banana split with extra, extra hot fudge without flinching; and how to fill out ridiculous applications that demand your true height and weight.

Here is **Big Girl Secret Tip #1:** *NEVER be truthful about your height/weight ratio; no self-respecting Big Girl tells all. It is imperative that you falsify this information, out of principle, to screw with the Powers That Be, particularly if you can bench press 400 pounds. Who's gonna challenge you?*

True Big Girls don't hide their largesse; they celebrate it. While occasionally they may reminisce about when they were a 1X instead of a 2X, trust me on this, it is not acceptable for a Big Girl to waste a lot of time moaning about days and dress sizes gone by. Now, thanks to Anne Kelly and her Junonia® crew, the Just My Size® people, Liz and Jane, and many other Big Girl clothiers, we are no longer obligated to run amok dressed in the latest striped offering from Omar the Tentmaker. It is a myth that Big Girls are lazy, that Big Girls can't play sports, and that Big Girls have no self-respect. Big Girls can be every bit as full of vitality and *joie de vivre* as the rest of the world's citizens, all wrapped up in a rather more statuesque package, or as a friend's grandma used to say, a *noticeable* body.

And for those of you who worry about us, and nag us to lose weight or get in shape, **let's review:** *I already know I'm fat, I don't need you to remind me. Do I go around telling you that you're going bald? Do I constantly remind you that you have bad taste in clothes? Do I incessantly relay to the world in your presence that you could sure stand to have those god-awful moles removed because they are just about the ugliest things I've ever seen, and you have such a pretty face?*

No, of course not. Big Girls are hyper-sensitive to the needs of other people because we crave the love of the world, the acceptance of our peers, and we wish to high heaven our family, especially great Aunt Sookie, would just shut up about it already, so we, therefore, avoid such uncouth tactics.

Big Girls of the world, you know who you are. It's not about height or weight. It's about attitude and getting our fair share. It's about feeling comfortable in our own skins, and wearing a bathing suit in public, despite the fact that the life-guard will whistle an Orca Alert every time we approach the ocean. It's about liking ourselves and our lives, and doing something about our circumstances when we don't. 'Nuf said. Now, for how to get there.

Chapter Two

Food & Its Procurement

Every Big Girl knows
the *Four Main Food Groups*
by heart:
1) Chocolate
2) Garlic
3) Red wine
   *(may substitute beer or
   other alcoholic beverages
   as needed)*
4) Dessert

For the grossly uneducated, God bless you and please allow me to point out the distinction between Food Group Number One, *Chocolate,* and Food Group Number Four, *Dessert: Chocolate* is an essential element. Our bodies require it. We need it to keep our internal gears moving smoothly. If chocolate is taken from us by force, things will get ugly and there will be hell to pay.

It is perfectly permissible to eat chocolate for breakfast, as a between-meal snack, as an appetizer, or as a main dish. Chocolate is an excellent tool to "close one's stomach," and is an excellent cure for toddler tantrums, the raging hormonal tirades of adolescents, PMS, peri-menopausal syndrome, menopause, Alzheimer's, and past-due electric bills. Trust me on this. Forget that banana hoodoo ... chocolate is nature's truly perfect food. If you don't believe me, try giving a banana to a menopausal woman who is having a hot flash and screaming at you to turn on the air conditioning, which is already set at 45 degrees.

On the other hand, *Dessert,* the plural of which is *stressed* spelled backwards, is a combination of ingredients that is presented with a flourish at the end of a meal. The best desserts, as any chef worth his big white hat knows, contain *chocolate,* but they remain distinctly in the *dessert* category, otherwise how could we, in good conscience and without a trace of guilt whatsoever, devour those delectable cocoa mints that the waiter places on the tray with the bill?

To further clarify a sticking point among culinary experts, *let's review:* it is absolutely *apropos* to eat an entire dessert whose fabric is cut solely from the chocolate cloth and then follow it with those little mints or a Triple-Fudge milkshake on the walk home, or both. Either way, your appetite is satisfied, your daily dose of nutritionally required chocolate is achieved, and you won't verbally abuse your partner or housemates for at least several hours, until your body again craves what it needs. *Our bodies, our selves* ... yeah, well, this body needs chocolate for itself, so get the hell out of my way, *pronto!*

Reader, be warned: there lurk among us some Big Girls who are extremely fussy about their chocolate. It must be unadulterated, without nuts, fruits, or fillings. It must be wrapped in gold foil and bear a foreign name with a half-dozen accent marks, making it virtually impossible for anyone on earth to properly pronounce. It must be kept in the freezer or baked into cookies. And then there's the *milk vs. dark* debate ... dark, sweet, and rich, like my men? Oh, sorry, that's about coffee. Really, let's get a life! Is there a *bad* form of chocolate? Yes, chocolate sauce that chemically transforms itself into a hard shell after you pour it on ice cream is the work of the devil. But seriously, does it matter how chocolate manifests itself, as long as that manifestation includes a one-way ticket into our open mouths? So get over yourselves and just eat a Hershey® bar, ok? And, to let the world know exactly what side of the butter fat highway you prefer, name your pet after a chocolate bar. You'll thank me for this, I promise.

We shall briefly address Food Groups Two and Three, because, let's face it, although they're every bit as essential as chocolate and dessert, they're not nearly as important. Without *Garlic* and *Red Wine*, we'd be forced to eat chocolate and dessert all day, and who would want to do that? *Stop it!* Put your hands down. *Garlic* needs no explanation, in my opinion. You can pull some of this stuff out of the ground, peel it, throw it in a pan, roast the hell out of it, and it tastes great on crackers. Not to mention *Garlic's Natural Health Benefits* ... experts say garlic is good for your digestion, lungs, blood pressure, circulation, plus it scares away vampires. Maybe so, but in addition to these wonderful traits, how many times have you fled the company of an unbearably boring gentleman simply by expelling a hefty wind from your garlic-infused lungs? I once had a date with *Mister Quadruple Lack of Personality from Hell.* Thank God he liked Italian, because that chef couldn't put enough garlic in the pasta to suit me. It was a blessedly brief evening, followed of course by chocolate, in the privacy of my own home.

Red Wine is useful, indeed. Like *Garlic,* it can alleviate any dire social situation through its miraculous soothing effects. Give me a male dinner companion whose toupee resembles the worn-out seat on your grandma's horsehair sofa and I'll show you exactly how *Red Wine* can turn the evening into a soirée that's more festive than the Cannes after-parties. The trick is to imbibe until you become giggly, wherein you feel completely at ease asking, *"Is that a Derby winner on your head or just a quarter horse?"* Hopefully Bad Toupee will pour you into a taxi by yourself, where you can indulge in all the mints you stole from the hostess stand while Bad Toupee complained about the bill and your garlic breath.

The Great Creator invented Garlic and Red Wine specifically for Big Girls. He knew that with our incredibly amazing Big Girl Zest for Life we'd be packin' away quite a bit of food, which in turn ratchets up the strain on the old ticker. But, *aha,* that's why He's the Great Creator. He made Garlic and Red Wine "heart-healthy" so we can eat as much as we like. Nutritional Experts of the World ... back at ya! *(We know you have a response, but right now we choose to ignore you and enjoy another glass of wine and a few cloves of garlic, ok?)*

Now that we've addressed the *Four Main Food Groups,* it's critical to review the all-important *Big Girl Dining Tips.* These are complex items that fall outside the simple *Four Main Food Group* categories, and because of my exhaustive, extensive research and life experience, you may now comfortably navigate your personal vessel through the *Sea of Big Girl Culinary Etiquette. (Man, that certainly was a bunch of b.s., wasn't it?)*

Let's review the Big Girl Dining Tips:

1) **Portion Size:** Who cares? And exactly what business is it of yours, anyway, unless you're coveting my dinner, waiting for me to utter those nasty, gnarly words that will *never,* I repeat *NEVER* issue from any self-respecting Big Girl's lips: *I'm too full to finish this.* Get your own plateful, you shameless hussy. Hey, you gonna eat that last tater tot?

2) **Snacks:** Eat them as often as you like, in any shape, form, or fashion. This is not a difficult concept to grasp.

3) **Finger Foods:** Avoid these at all costs, ladies. Picture this, if you will ... you're in an obscenely expensive restaurant being treated to dinner because you're the Client (no one would ever believe a Big Girl could actually get a *date,* so work with me on this). You're dressed to the nines in a Big Girl Suit and Big Girl Shoes and you're looking fabulous, dahling, fabulous. But it is *raving lunacy* to believe that you can disguise yourself as anything but the Big Girl you are. Sure, you command the eyes of everyone in the restaurant. They're all waiting for your panty hose to split open at the crotch, your blouse to pop a button, or for you to, horror of horrors, lick your fingers. So avoid the finger foods. We all look *trés* more *chic* when holding a fork or spoon, or idly cradling a wine glass, deep in thought about what's on the dessert tray.

   And never, never, eat a corn dog in public, no matter what the circumstances. Unless of course the corn dogs are presented as *heavy hors d'oeuvres,* a concept that is particularly confusing to Big Girls. Today's moronic social practice states that *heavy hors d'oeuvres* substitute for a meal. Strictly speaking, every Big Girl knows that if it's not a full, three-course meal, it ain't no meal at all, and a few measly pieces of chicken on a skewer just don't cut it, ok?

4) **Gravy as a Vegetable:** I heartily recommend that all Big Girls adopt this time-honored tradition from the South into their personal eating habits. Gravy may also be counted as a *Side Dish,* if it contains little pieces of sausage. Let's clarify here, shall we? *Any gravy you can see through is not really gravy, ok?* It's a waste of time and an effort by the chef to

dispose of surplus meat drippings *(TRANSLATION: HE'S CHEAP)*, so let's stop kidding ourselves with the *au jus* crap and just bring me some thick-as-a-brick gravy I can sink my teeth into and dredge my biscuits in, please.

5) **Peer Support is Critical:** One of my absolute Best Pals in the world owns an ice cream store. This is a great friendship, let me tell you!

6) **Develop Your Personal Nutritional Plan:** Every creature on earth needs nourishment to exist, and each of us has unique, personal, nutritional needs. The hat trick for Big Girls is to spend time to adequately and thoroughly assess your individual nutritional profile; I'd say three minutes is plenty long enough. The key is to figure out how much of the *Four Main Food Groups* you require to avoid red-lining the Bitch Meter on a daily basis. Write it down if you must, then commit that puppy to memory, and let 'er rip!

7) **Staying On Plan When Eating Out:** This is a toughie, particularly for those Big Girls who demand regimented programs with charts and graphs and pep talks; those weak souls among us who are infinitely tied to counting something so mundane as "points." Point counting is socially limiting, plus it's a total Big Girl faux pas to holler, *"How many points is an entire box of Krispy Kreme® doughnuts?"* at an important breakfast meeting. I know for a fact that this point thing is nothing but a scam by nutritionists to make Big Girls suffer in restaurants. A friend once told me that the only way to arrive at accurate point levels is to take the food's points, double them and add 30. Which means that one's acceptable Total Daily Point Intake consists of a half-

slice of wheat toast and three ounces of weak tea. This may be fine if you're an actress who craves a concentration camp-starved body, but for me, *not!*

Here are my **Big Girl, No-Fail Suggestions for Staying On Plan When Eating Out:**

a)   Politely inform the waiter, "Look, let's skip the salad and entrée. Just cut to the chase and bring me the dessert cart, ok?"

b)   When you're on the go, living the Exciting Big Girl Life, you can save an enormous amount of calories by pairing a Diet Coke® with that sackful of Krystals you just ordered.

c)   Instead of having a Jelly Doughnut, to the tune of 450 points, why not satisfy yourself with 400 celery sticks and 18 glasses of water? *I really don't think so. Get me my Big Girl bowie knife ...*

d)   Every Big Girl knows that mashed potatoes with the skins <u>on</u> are far more nutritionally sound than no mashed potatoes whatsoever. And no self-respecting Big Girl would dream of eating mashed potatoes without **Gravy as a Vegetable** *(see previous)*. We're talking trace elements of iron in those potato skins, something every Big Girl needs for good health, and you naturally take in more trace elements with a double helping, so load up.

e)   Twinkies® possess an amazing shelf life, an asset for Big Girls on the Go. Let's say you're going on a hike in the wilds of Ecuador (work with me here, maybe you pulled the Big Girl slot on *Survivor* or something). You could take extreme, inadvisable risks to your health and well-being by eating the large variety of local fruits, vegetables, and worms in the rain forest and spend every waking moment of the next three weeks in the latrine. Or, you could instead partake of your own personal, hidden stash of Twinkies, which not only fill you up, but might stop you up, and *let's review,* there's not exactly an abundance of toilet paper in the jungle, now, is there?

f) Salad is most definitely *NOT* an entrée. It's *SALAD.* It is physically impossible to eat only *SALAD* and not die from starvation that very same day, with one exception: a taco salad at any Mexican restaurant. I once had the brilliant idea that I could stay on plan and eat a taco salad, because hell, it was SALAD! It had lettuce and tomatoes and refried beans … beans are low-fat! I was so proud of myself I did the happy dance all afternoon until I read in the point booklet that the total points for the taco salad's fried shell, sour cream, and cheese alone exhausted all my combined points for the next three weeks. I'm warning you, if you just eat *SALAD,* when those starvation symptoms hit you, you'll beat a path to the nearest snack machine so fast it will set your shoes on fire. In a quarter-feeding frenzy you'll smash every one of the buttons on that machine until you've emptied its contents and you're sitting on the floor in the break room awash in little wrappers. If you simply must have a *SALAD,* then pile on some kind of meat, for God's sakes; and a truckload of cheese, croutons, bacon, and full-fat, bleu cheese dressing. Order it alongside the *Double Cheeseburger Combo Plate* to save face in the break room later. I mean, we all need our veggies, right? *Stay on plan, ladies!*

g) When faced with the challenge of entertaining business guests, all bets are off as you place your own nutritional needs on the back burner in favor of your client's. Therefore it is perfectly acceptable to set your points chart on fire and flush it down the commode. **A Case in Point:** Once while on business in Milan, I committed an unpardonable sin: I skipped breakfast. The fact that I was having a war with the front desk and they turned off the electricity in my room to make me late for my meeting is another story for another time. *So.* I presented myself at my customer's office, whereupon he offered me a demitasse of espresso. I promptly drank it, in an exercise of international espresso-drinking goodwill, and then excused myself to throw up. This went on for several hours, until I had the *delirium tremens* and very bad breath, when finally, Sandro, my customer, exclaimed, "Now is lunch?" Yes, *NOW would be an excellent time for lunch, because, gee, it's only three o'clock in the afternoon. I've had fourteen cups of espresso and thrown up twenty-five pounds! I need some food!* My customer and his colleagues then hosted what I'm sure they believed to be an extremely festive party, *á la* your garden-variety Fellini movie. After a forty-five minute journey that resembled nothing short of a ride in the trunk of a car straight down the side of a rocky mountain, we arrived at a local bistro where Sandro insisted on ordering the house specialty, my personal favorite, spaghetti. After much flourish and attention from the restaurant owner, and very near to four in the afternoon, we had *lunch*. *At last*, I thought to myself, being the Polite Big Girl Who Never Rocks the Boat that I am, *I can eat something and feel better.* Wrong, again. It was spaghetti, all right ... squid-fish-octopus spaghetti. Presented to a stomach burned by espresso, bile, and the traffic in Milan. This delectable dish featured enormous body parts from creatures that ordinarily reside in the sea and are not at all meant to be served with spaghetti to a carsick American woman. There was no tomato sauce, no garlic cheese toast or breadsticks, no parmesan cheese in the little green shaker can ... good grief, what kind of Italian did these people *eat?* This was my Absolute Bar None Worst Food Day in the History of the Universe.

That evening, upon arrival at the Milan Airport, I overcame near-starvation, trekked my Big Girl International Businesswoman's Butt over to duty free and purchased three pounds of Swiss chocolate and a large hunk of bread. I ate every bit of it in the lounge while waiting for my plane. To this day, I can't bear to look at a squid, and I'm convinced that, although this took place ten years ago, I still haven't gained back all the weight I lost that day in Milan. My sole consolation was that I didn't have to eat a bowlful of garlic eels at National Eel Day, like my International Traveler Big Girl Friend, when she visited customers in Japan. Those poor, misguided people think that an appropriate snack is an eel head on a stick. Her experience was the sole exception to *Garlic as a Food Group* ... always travel with Twinkies *(see #5 above)* or Peanut M&M®s.

h) Last, but not least, I cannot overstate the magnitude of ice cream as a dairy source. You've seen the milk mustache commercials. You know the drill. We all need more calcium. A medical expert recently commented that in the Great Order of the Solar System, our Maker didn't intend for grown-ups to drink milk. *Finally!* Every Big Girl worth her weight in Chunky Monkey® knows that ice cream contains calcium and that we're much better off eating our FDA-approved allowance of said calcium in a bowl of ice cream instead of drinking it from a glass. Really, do the FDA people live in a hut?

Big Girls are food procurement experts. We know where to buy that dreamy Italian chocolate spread, Nutella®, and where to find the perfect Scottish shortbread to go with it. We know the location of the best fried chicken or barbecue in town. We know where the nearest all-night diner is and, most importantly, we belong to those monster warehouse stores, because it is imperative that we be able to purchase a five-gallon drum of chocolate syrup and a six-pack of bundt cakes on a whim. Here are **A Few Useful Big Girl Grocery Shopping Tricks** that I'll share with you:

1) *Avoid fit-and-trim shoppers at all costs.* They're dying to inspect your cart to see what it is you eat that makes you such a Big Girl. *No wonder she can't fit through Aisle Seven, with all those Ding Dongs® and Little Debbies®!*

2) *A double package of adult diapers can conceal most snack foods, if the snack foods are properly grouped within the cart and the diapers placed on top.* You'll need the diapers

in a few years, but at that point you won't be able to remember to buy them, so trust me, stock up *now*.

3) *Conceal your layer cake habit* by having the Bakery Lady inscribe it with *"Happy Birthday Emily."* No one will be the wiser.

4) *Purchase cough syrup with your binge items.* Who's to say you don't have a person at home who is near death, and you, Kind Big Girl that you are, have gone forth to procure sustenance to stave off the Grim Reaper? Casually comment to the checker, *"He's really sick. I bought a few of his favorites to see if he can keep anything down."* What a woman! Pass me the tissues!

Never challenge a Big Girl to a Food Shopping Scavenger Hunt, unless you have a penchant for being whipped like a meringue and left to die on the sidewalk … you can't win. And don't stand in front of the latest meat-and-three in town on opening day, honey … you'll be trampled under the Parade of the Self-Appointed Big Girl Food Critics as they compete for the first slice of the Double Fudge Pie.

It might seem logical to non-Big Girl types to ask, "Why aren't more Big Girls caterers or restaurateurs?" Sure, let the fatties run the food business! *Let's review:* Big Girls aren't caterers because we'd eat all the profits! We may be hefty, but we're not stupid. We know a losing proposition when we see one. And really, who the hell wants to stand on their feet all day, cookin' up grub for strangers? If I'm gonna swell my varicose veins to make a meatloaf, baby, you can be sure it ain't gonna be for someone I don't know!

Now that we've settled that issue, let's move on to **Big Girl**

Secret Tip #2: *It is perfectly acceptable and expected for Big Girls to eat on the sly. Candy bars fit nicely under the magazines in your nightstand and behind the feminine hygiene products under the vanity.*

If you have teenagers, particularly if they are of the football-playing variety, it is imperative to identify your private Fail-Safe Food Hiding Place for Emergencies. Smart Big Girls take great pains to calculate exact distances from various convenience stores to their place of residence, to routinely enjoy a Payday® or other delicacy in its entirety while driving home. Briefcases make excellent trash cans, by the way.

A Case in Point: Let's say a Big Girl, we'll call her Daisy, goes to the grocery store to do her weekly shopping. But it has not been a good day for Daisy. Her husband abruptly decided to stay home to "be with her" while the kids are at school. He politely suggests they take a walk together, maybe get some exercise, to help her stay on track with her new diet. Daisy is *pissed.* She had intended to get a massage and a facial and a root job, then meet her girlfriends for lunch *(TRANSLA-TION: DESSERT),* thus, exercising with her husband is, needless to say, *not* her idea of a good time. Daisy informs her spouse that the pantry is bare, and although he offers to go to the grocery store for her, a veritable Saint of a Man, Daisy declines his offer because she knows it is time to activate *Emergency Plan B.*

At the grocery store, Daisy does her shopping in roughly thirty seconds, then steers toward the festive In-Store Bakery section. This haven of sugar-coated, frosted confections is surely the cure for Daisy's bad-day blues. Daisy ponders several selections for the better part of ten minutes, then places a delightfully enticing tray of cherry turnovers into her cart. Now every full-fledged Big Girl knows you can't eat cherry turnovers without chocolate milk, so Daisy heads for the dairy aisle and grabs a handy pint. For one near-fatal second she ponders the total number of points one might rack up if one consumes four cherry turnovers and a pint of chocolate milk in a single sitting, but she is saved by the ring of her cell phone. After completing her call, Daisy deftly instructs the sack boy to place the turnovers and the chocolate milk in a separate bag, then phones her husband as the sack boy loads the groceries into her ultra-large sport utility vehicle.

"Hi, hon. It's me. It's a madhouse here, I'll be a little while longer. See ya soon, *bye!*"

Satisfied that she has adequately pacified her exercise-obsessed husband for a few extra minutes, Daisy drives to the local soccer field and selects a prime parking spot at the very back of the lot. It's her favorite parking spot simply because it is shaded by a very large tree and out of sight from prying eyes. Daisy turns the radio to her favorite Oldies station, pops open the cherry turnovers and the chocolate milk, and *POOF,* just like magic, Daisy's Bad Day disappears into a cherry-filling-and-chocolate-milk-laden fantasy.

After thoroughly enjoying her midday treat and its recuperative effects, Daisy glances at her watch and decides to head home. No nasty telltale turnover trash for her ... Daisy bebops over to a waste can at the end of the soccer field and deposits all traces of her snack inside. After a couple of quick brushes to her chest to remove any crumbs, Daisy feels like herself again, invigorated by a sugar rush and certain she can face the rest of the day with her homebound husband, even if exercise is involved.

On those rare occasions when Daisy is unable to venture out to the grocery store to find sugared relief from the exhaustion she faces in her demanding role as a pampered housewife, she has *Emergency Plan C.* In her garage, Daisy keeps an extra refrigerator. And an extra freezer. Although she rationalized these purchases to her husband by claiming, *"The children need extra drinks in the summer,"* Daisy has the *Power of the Stash.* She knows this time-tested fact of the Big Girl Lifestyle: Twinkies freeze quite well, thaw quickly, and if you keep your freezer well-stocked, no one will ever find them hidden amongst the frozen vegetables, due to a **Universal Truism of Life:** *The odds that a Non-Mom Humanoid will actually move something in the freezer in hopes of locating a desired food substance are directly proportional to that Non-Mom Humanoid's ability to breathe.* It just ain't gonna happen.

So, Big Girls and all you aspiring Big Girl Wanna-bes out there, get yourself an extra fridge, an extra freezer, and find a secret parking spot between the grocery store and a trash can. And don't forget to note the location of every drive-thru in town … you never know when you might have five minutes to pick up some fries.

Chapter Three

Exercise & Its Avoidance

To say that I loathe exercise is to say that a sucking chest wound is hazardous to one's health. Exercise in any shape, form, or fashion is such a detestable concept to me I can barely bring myself to venture into a sporting goods store. I will, however, go so far as to extol at length the virtues of spandex running shorts and their ability to meld to one's expanding thighs.

On those rare occasions in my life when I embraced exercise with every ounce of Big Girl Passion I could physically muster, I can truly say that it changed me and that I felt much better for having done it. But the thought of getting out of a warm bed on a cold winter morning before the sun has poked its bright yellow head above the surface of the frozen earth, just to strap on fourteen layers of clothes and wheeze myself around the neighborhood, is abhorrent.

I have asthma and, although it is now controlled by no less than a barrel of cutting-edge medications, until I was a teenager it was difficult for me to do anything remotely sport-like without enduring an asthma attack. Of course, we now know that asthma is God's revenge on those elite few who possess genius-level intelligence, *so aren't you jealous?* Until I was about fifteen, I hated gym and all its ill-fitting accoutrements with a passion. At first my mom's notes excusing me from gym were well-founded, based on the severity of my asthma. Then, like all Extremely Clever Big Girls, I discovered that I could manipulate my mom and the gym teacher like nobody's business, and from that day forward, exercise was not a word that inhabited either my vocabulary or my daily routine.

Exercise is typically not on the Favorite Hobby List of Big Girls, with the exception of the Amazon Big Girls, the lucky ones talented enough to excel at basketball, volleyball, and other sports where size is an advantage. Let's face it, there's not much flab on female athletes, but that's a sad topic for another day. For most Big Girls, gym is one of the Absolute Terrors of Life, and a school career of bad gym experiences undoubtedly produces something on the order of Anna Nicole Smith. I remember well the embarrassment of being the last person selected for the relay race teams in grade school.

Why, I yearned to ask my gym teacher, would I willingly don a polyester uniform that fit me, in my overweight glory, with the adherence of a feed sack? Why would I volunteer to subject myself to the President's Fitness Test, as if I gave a rat's ass how many push-ups and sit-ups I could perform before I puked? These are not skills I need to excel in life! Teach me about proper snacking at major sporting events. Instruct me on the finer points of lifting a twelve-pack versus an entire case of beer. And don't get me started on the Big Girl's worst nightmare ... dodge ball. I hated dodge ball and it hated me. Big Girls make excellent dodge ball targets. I can still feel the terrible sting of that red leather ball on my chubby legs as my classmates hurled it at me over and over again.

When I was a teenager, I actually enjoyed tennis and basketball, at least the backyard varieties. I could hold my own at both within the neighborhood and my Big Girl Peer Group. I participated in walkathons for charity, but that was solely motivated by the number of cute boys in tow. In my twenties, during my exhilarating career as an accounting clerk at a public utility, I surprised everyone at the company picnic with my prowess at volleyball. My slam-dunk serves won the game for our team, and for about a three-minute period, I knew what great athletes feel when they've captured The Prize. I had to stay home from work the next day, however, because my right arm would not move. But, doggone it, I excelled, if only briefly, as a Big Girl Athlete.

In those rare and brief periods of time when Bunkie Big Girl Momentarily Left the Planet and her Senses Behind, I signed up for Jazzercise® classes and joined fitness clubs. Jazzercise can be a lot of fun, especially if you enjoy making a complete and total fool of yourself to music. I worked very hard in those sessions, though it's difficult to know if I received more benefit from the actual exercise or the effort required to suppress my belly laughter at the ill-timed, jerky movements of my classmates. I know that most White Chicks don't have much in the way of Rhythm, but come on, we were exercising to Kool and the Gang ... how hard can it be to kick your leg to that backbeat? There was one woman who, God love her, was always at least thirty seconds behind everyone else in the routine. On more than one occasion I narrowly missed suffering an aneurysm while trying not to laugh out loud.

Of course, I cheated in Jazzercise just like I cheated in gym … the floor exercises were unfit for human participation. If God had intended us to distort our bodies in that manner, he would have given us tails and a rubber spine. I cleverly relived my grade school gym days and *pretended* to do the full exercise, while in reality I sort of laid around on the mat, occasionally waving my legs in the air and groaning when appropriate.

I escaped unnoticed except for one nosy gal in pink spandex who apparently thought she was the Jazzercise Police. I always caught her staring at me in my state of blissful repose, and believe me, for her to stare at me while she maintained the Torture Position was no small feat, that gal was in great shape. But, I had the last laugh, you betcha. Now, I don't ordinarily poke fun at people for the way they dress … ok, at least I have the good manners not to do it within earshot. Anyway, the Jazzercise Policewoman apparently didn't know much about undies. Everyone with an ounce of sense knows you don't wear big, white, granny undies beneath a form-fitting pink spandex leotard. To say that the Jazzercise Policewoman had a visible panty line is to say that Elvis sold a few records.

My forays to the fitness club were no picnic, either. Good grief, I needed a mechanic's license just to change the weight levels on the machines. Then I prayed the machines wouldn't fall on top of me and crush me to death while I counted my belly rolls in the full-sized mirror three inches from my face. It is safe to say that my all-time favorite, strength-training exercise is the Twelve-Ounce Curl, preferably in a Bar of My Choosing. If that doesn't do it for you, you can always go to the monster warehouse store and, after making an appropriate purchase for your personal weight-training program, perform Chee.tos® Super Size Canister Lifts in the privacy of your parked car *(remember **Big Girl Secret Tip #2**).*

Last year on New Year's day, I decided it was time to take control of my life, words I frequently utter and words my husband has learned to dread. We made yet another pact to diet and exercise, and, in an extremely rare and feeble moment, I allowed a friend, a Big Girl Who Exercises, to talk me into training for a half-marathon in our town. I had four months to get in shape and be able to walk thirteen miles. My husband, who could easily run to Peru and back without breaking a sweat, agreed to help.

For the first two or three days, I had big fun. I visited the Absolute Best Sports Training Store in Town, according to my girlfriend, the expert. There I paid top dollar for the Absolute Best Running Shoes Money Can Buy, and believe me, money can buy an awful lot for what I paid for those shoes. Not only were these terrific running shoes, they were Big Girl Special Running Shoes, featuring extra support for Big Girl impact, I guess, because my pace could never be described as running, by any stretch of the imagination.

After shoes, it was necessary to obtain the right socks. God forbid I should get any blisters! Add the purchase of a fanny pack, exercise tights to brave the winter weather, a new windbreaker, a sports bra that gave rise to a brand new body part I fondly refer to as the "Uniboob," a must-have sports watch complete with chronometer and lap timer *(as if)*, and an MP3 player to help me find my groove during training sessions.

Now you non-exercising Big Girls are probably saying, *"Girl, I bet you had a major chafe-thing going on, uh-huh!"* Wrong, sistuh. I possessed the Secret of Body Glide®. This amazing little tool is what set me apart from the amateurs, I guarantee. First, seeing as how I was at the Absolute Best Sports Training Store in Town, I forked over what the clerk believed to be a reasonable amount but to me represented one week's wages, for a four-inch stick of Body Glide. Before suiting up for the Hunt, before strapping on those spandex shorts and the Uniboob holder, I took that little Body Glide dispenser and rubbed it between various and sundry body parts that tend to overlap and collide with each other. Please don't make me spell it out, you know *exactly* what I'm talkin' about! It's why Big Girls don't take long walks on the beach after their shorts get wet. We'd rather not do the Bowlegged Cowboy Saunter out of necessity for the next three days, ok?

I was all set, to the tune of several hundred dollars. I looked the part, I acted the part, I felt the part ... the part of my legs that ached constantly, that's what I mostly felt. I walked and trained and followed my schedule. I was so invincible it was sickening. I even ate the right foods and drank three thousand gallons of water per day and, miracle of miracles, I *lost weight.*

The day of the half-marathon arrived. The thrill of the chase and the rush of the competitors overtook me as we Walkers clamored for a spot of our own among the Runners during the first minutes of the race. I was pumped, despite being swiftly passed by several Super-Women Runners. You know the type: those ultra-thin, boobless, skinny-legged wonders we affectionately call Greyhounds. I'm serious. You can see *daylight* between their thighs! This is not *normal!* They could most likely run to Ethiopia and back and then survive on a cucumber and a cup of water. In fact, I think they originated in Ethiopia, where dining is unfortunately an annual occurrence. More power to 'em, you go girls! Just don't step on my fragile toes on your way to the finish line.

I trucked along beside my husband, visualizing my photo on the front page of the newspaper, *FAT CHICK BEATS PACK TO WIN HALF-MARATHON,* when it happened ... I had to pee. I won't bore you with details, but let it suffice to say that I wasted ten minutes waiting for a bathroom, despite the fact that fellow marathoners were unabashedly peeing out in the open, immediately downstream from the gas station car wash. In total frustration I calculated that I would now be forced to *run,* not walk, the next few miles in order to make up time and receive a finisher's medal. This horrifying conclusion occurred at *Mile Two* of a thirteen-mile event. I promptly decided then and there to quit, go to Waffle House®, and watch the results on TV. Had I bothered to wear my expensive chronometer, however, I would have realized that I'd made a serious math error. There was still plenty of time to negotiate the finish line. But I convinced myself that I had already lost, and in my best Big Girl Whiner Voice, began to Make Excuses, which is, by the way, a favorite Big Girl activity.

My dear, sweet, loving husband turned into The Competitive Sports Jerk from Hades. He forcibly dragged my Big Girl Fat Ass up and down a series of the most strenuous hills you've ever laid eyes on. We caught up with my girlfriend and her husband, and the three of them took turns pushing my Load of Lard up one hill and down another for the next two and a half hours. Not only were my feet killing me, my lungs wracked with pain as I attempted to breathe, and my pride was under attack. My girlfriend, the Big Girl Who Exercises, didn't break a sweat. She was singing and clapping and playing the *Let's Motivate Everyone* and *Isn't This a Perfect Party Game.* I wanted to kill her, except that I couldn't move my arms. This brings me to **Big Girl Secret Tip #3:** *Never pay good money to participate in an organized sports event where you are expected to do something in less than three weeks.*

The biggest mistake I made that day was to drink pure Gatorade® at a water stop. Well, excuse me. *Stop? HELL,* you can't *stop* after you've been walking for three hours continuously! Your legs would just crumple underneath you, so you're forced to grab a little paper cup of liquid as you walk by and try to drink it without spilling most of it on your person, then hope to God that some of it makes its way over your lips into your thirst-wracked body, so you won't die a terrible death of dehydration in public as everyone else tramples over you. Not being an experienced Big Girl Athlete, I was a Gatorade newbie, having never touched the stuff, which really works if you're used to it. But instead of cutting it with water so as not to freak out my virgin Gatorade tummy, I gulped that puppy right down. *Big mistake.* My stomach immediately protested and sent the Gatorade right back up my throat. My Big Girl Friend Who Exercises yells, "Hey! Did you just drink straight Gatorade on an empty stomach? Didn't I tell you not to do that? Didn't you read the MANUAL?"

To quote Steve Martin, my favorite comedian, *"I forgot."* What does she of the Clap and Sing Your Way to the Finish Line Club tell me to do now? "Drink lots of water, it will help. Try to breathe, it will help. Picture yourself climbing Mount Everest, it will help. Here, suck on this mint, it will help." *She lied.* Nothing helped, especially the Mount Everest idea. I could only visualize my dead, frozen body sticking out of the side of Mount Everest, while my girlfriend and her husband and my husband happily climbed over me with their Sherpas, toting ice cream sundaes. *And they found her there, frozen solid, with a bird perched on the icy doughnut she grasped in her blue hand ...*

For the rest of the race my legs ached and burned. My toes were numb and my stomach roiled. But I could not stop walking. I began to hallucinate ... *I'm walking and I can't stop ... I might never stop walking ... there's another hill, I'm going to die*

on that hill ... there's my friend being cheerful, I HATE her.
There's my husband, I hate him, too. They're in this together for
the insurance money. STOP CLAPPING AND SINGING!
STOP IT! Just leave me alone in my misery. No, wait. Here comes
another hill ... grab my arm and pull my Big Girl Ass up to the
top ... don't you DARE leave me here to DIE on this hill, you ass-
holes! Is there chocolate at that water stop? I think I'm going to die
and no one cares. Look at that skinny bitch in the pink running
suit ... it's the Jazzercise Policewoman! But HA! Her big, white,
granny undies are flapping in the breeze! Thank you, Lord, for this
uplifting moment! I may be near death, but at least my under-
wear is fully contained in my shorts!

To add insult to injury, the last mile of the half-marathon
was uphill. It was obscene. I had long ago exhausted the best
of my Big Girl Cuss Words and was now simply moving by
rote. I'm quite certain I endured a Near-Death Experience and
hovered above my own body, waiting to limp into the light.
When my girlfriend cheerfully suggested we all hold hands as
we crossed the finish line, I wanted to ram my expensive athletic shoe up her Big Girl Who Exercises behind in the worst
way, but I didn't have it in me, because in truth, she helped get
me my medal, and I do owe her something for that.

We crossed the line and received our medals. I cried and
she cried and her husband cried and my husband cried and
hugged me, and then we proceeded to the Finish Corral, where
I promptly ate everything in sight. True to form, food provided
me comfort. You have not lived until you have personally witnessed five thousand gigantic, sugar-topped blueberry muffins
waiting for you in open boxes, calling for you to adopt them
as part of your personal nutritional intake. Sure, there were
other things for the marathoners to eat, like yogurt and
oranges and bananas *(refer to previous comment on bananas)*,

but I made a beeline for the blueberry muffins, as best as a person who is hobbling with numb feet and blistered toes after surviving a near-death experience, can.

My recovery from the half-marathon took three weeks. I immediately went home and swallowed several surplus narcotics, undoubtedly left over from some previous overweight-related injury and left my husband to deal with his own physical misery, our son, and two dogs. After more narcotics and a few days later, I could walk, though only in open-toed sandals. I created quite a stir as my friends casually asked, *"Um,* excuse me, but are your toes *oozing?"* Yes, I was now a Big Girl with a Medal and Oozing Toes. The fun part was when the toenails turned a most interesting shade of brown and fell off. I proudly displayed them to my friend, the Big Girl Who Exercises, when she asked if I wanted to sign up for another half-marathon in a few months. It worked like a charm.

So my Personal and Professional Big Girl Advice to you, gentle reader, is fully contained in **Big Girl Secret Tip #4:** *Exercise is what you make it. Channel surfing burns calories, as does working crossword puzzles and screwing the lid back on the peanut butter jar. You need proof? Look at Richard Simmons and tell me he's not a hottie in his "Before" photos! Do you really want to hop around half-naked to songs your grandmother enjoyed? No, I didn't think so.*

Chapter Four

The Unkindness of Strangers

Human beings are so confounding. We can project ourselves as the ultimate in sweetness and light. Yet, in the very next breath we can transform into a combination of Attila the Hun and Medusa. I admit I have never lingered on the sunny side of the sweet meter. I have a big mouth and an acerbic wit; however, I do believe I have the good graces to make my comments either in the silence of my own mind or in the privacy of a very noisy bar where only my best friends can hear me.

That doesn't mean I won't give you a blazingly honest opinion if you insist on it, but because my mother raised me to be a Big Girl Who is, Above All Things, *Nice*, it isn't in my behavior bag to insult people without provocation. I do believe, however, that I am the exception to the rule, as the following *TRUE STORIES* will confirm.

Recently I was minding my own business in the hair salon that I have frequented for quite a while. The proprietor runs a great shop, a place like the one Dolly Parton operated in *Steel Magnolias,* where half the town goes to get their new dos and nails done. It's nothing fancy, but let me tell you, they are hair experts. There is nothing these gals can't do … classic, big Southern hair, Mid-town Atlanta purple hair, J. Lo hair … they do it *all,* in every shade of the rainbow, and they do it *well.* I could get my hair cut virtually anywhere, I'm very low-maintenance, however I pick up the most fantastical dialogue for my fiction novels in this salon. The people who work there have always been extremely nice to me, which is surprising in itself, because I am not the kind of gal folks warm up to.

So. I'm sitting there, patiently waiting for my haircut, flipping through a magazine. One of the operators is glued to a television that is tuned to a reality exposé program. Today's show features the illuminating tale of three young people, barely in their twenties, who are absolutely convinced they require plastic surgery. One boy, whose body resembled a stunning combination of Adonis, Charles Atlas, and Sylvester Stallone in the good days, insisted that he could not live one more second without calf implants. How he could see that he *needed* calf implants through the numerous tattoos on his person, I'm not sure, but who am I to question the Dumbing of America?

In any case, one woman on the program, who was morbidly obese and likely weighed over 400 pounds, decided to undergo gastric bypass surgery. At this point the beauty operator, who is ordinarily a sweet person, turned to her colleague, *not two feet* from where I sat in all my Glorious Big Girlness, and said, "How much do you think she *weighs? Good God,* how does somebody *get* like that? I was *never* very good at guessing a fat person's weight. Now my *sister,* who is *BIG,* I mean, she feels bad because me and my other sister are slim, she is *BIG,* she probably tops 250. You know what my husband would say about that girl on TV? He'd say if you put her on a treadmill and taped a candy bar to the handlebars and forced her to walk off the same amount of calories that are in that candy bar, she'd step off that treadmill and say, *'Hey! I don't want that candy bar now, because look how hard I just worked!'* Lemme tell ya, that's how you lose weight, what's so hard about it?"

Ok, when did I suddenly become *invisible* and when did *you* become the All-Knowing Psychic Problem-Solver to the World's Fat People? If you're sizing up the woman on TV, I figure you're silently assessing me as well. Call me paranoid, but I've lived the Life of a Big Girl for too long and I know how this stuff works. Now if my friend, the Big Girl Who Doesn't Take Jack Off Anybody, had been there, she wouldn't have blinked. She'd have stood up and faced that beautician and said, *"HEY!* I was never very good at guessing how much of a *MORONIC JUDGMENTAL TWIT* you might be. Maybe we should strap your tongue to a hamster wheel and see how long it takes for you to vocalize an apology!"

But, like I said, I'm the Big Girl Who is, Above All Things, *Nice,* so I continued to flip through my magazine and ignore the lot of them, although my insides broiled. After my haircut, I drove straight home and wrote this chapter; *HA,* the last word!

My Big Girl Friend Who Takes Exotic Vacations tells a story that, to this day, gives me nightmares. She visited one of those combination All-Inclusive Resort-*slash*-Third-World-Country places, where the evening's entertainment was to learn to dance the merengue. All this merengue dancing led to an Adult Scavenger Hunt, and they needed a belt. My Big Girl Friend Who Takes Exotic Vacations can count on one hand the times in her life when she has worn a belt. Unfortunately, this was one of them. She unlashed that puppy, swung it onstage, and the emcee promptly shouted, *"WHOA, NELLY,* this belt is *HUGE!* It's obviously a *woman's* belt, but it shouldn't be!" It took my Friend three visits from room service and a bottle of tequila to recuperate. Let me tell you, she said that was a *goooood* bottle of tequila, because the next morning, she told the emcee exactly where to go and how to get there!

Which brings me to **Big Girl Secret Tip #5:** *Forget the Girl Scouts. "Be prepared" for Big Girls means that we should always have an Acidic Comeback or Insulting Gesture up our Plus-sized sleeves. Trust me on this. Stretch those middle fingers, practice rolling those eyes and shaking that head, and attain your personal best time for the Big Girl Hand-on-Your-Hip-and-Finger-Pointing Event.*

Let's review: A former colleague of mine, an admitted Anorexic, used to sit in my office and pretend to discuss business. In reality, we waited for the end of the day, just like in school when we waited for the bell to ring. As college-educated adults, fully cognizant of the fact that we'd look ridiculous in our expensive navy suits and pumps if we raced each other to the front door, we calmly spent the last fifteen minutes or so of each day swapping idle chat about the weather or our social calendars, albeit with one eye fixed on the clock. We maintained this charade, and it worked fine for us. Anyway, she, being an Anorexic, and I, being a Big Girl, bonded. She always joked that in the Eating Disorders Treatment Facility, the Anorexics and the Overeaters constantly devised food swaps that were more intricately planned than the escape from

Alcatraz. She carved holes in the walls of her room to stash her unwanted but ultra-valuable dinner rolls, and then traded them through a series of mysterious accomplices for a full-length mirror. Well, in any case, we were buds. Along with several other clock-watchers we formed an unofficial Anorexic and Big Girls Work Club with requisite meetings most afternoons.

A newly hired Powder-Puff Girl emerged on the scene. My standard definition of a Powder-Puff Girl is not fit for print, even in what has already become a potty-mouthed excuse for literature, as my grandmother would say, so I'll revise it a bit. You know the Powder-Puff Girl: Her hair is just right, her makeup never slides down her face, she wears the height of fashion, and you never *ever* see her in the same outfit twice. Her body is toned, her teeth are dazzling, and she has a tan in January but no visible tan lines or wrinkles. She sports "estate" jewelry made from precious gems that at auction could feed a Third World nation, and cocktail rings that I swear she bought from a television hawker. *(What is it with "cocktail rings," any-way? Maybe you're supposed to drool at your ring instead of the food at a fancy party?)*

To add insult to injury, Powder-Puff's fiancé bought her the cutest convertible sports car, *isn't it cute?* Just when you think you can overlook her perky, Powder-Puffiness, find the goodness beneath the designer silk, she cuts you to the quick and steals your customers. In short, we hate her, don't we? *Yes, of course we do.*

Powder-Puff Girl was at the top of our hit list primarily due to a comment she made one spring day. I swear I am not making this up. There we all stood, working women of the world around the water cooler, when a Man in Sales interrupted our extremely important exchange about the Hunks of

ER, and complimented Powder-Puff Girl on her new fire-engine red, oh-so-tailored business suit. She flashed her teeth, tossed her glossy hair, and said casually, "Oh, *thanks so much!* This was my Easter outfit, isn't it cute? Don't you love it when your mommy takes you shopping and buys you a new Easter outfit? It's a little big, I usually take a size *two,* but it was the last one on the rack and I just had to have it!"

We hated her from that day forward. Other co-workers soon caught the Clue Bus as well, when Powder-Puff Girl wore out her welcome and she played dirty pool one too many times. The bloom finally cascaded down her Powder-Puff Girl face, and she evolved into the Raging Ex-Small Town Beauty Queen from Hell. She gained weight, became pudgy, *and we loved every minute of it!* Each day, the Anorexic and Big Girls Work Club traded the latest news about the Fall of Powder-Puff Girl. I'm admitting to the world here that I gossiped. I did. *And I enjoyed it.* But I never ever said anything to Powder-Puff Girl's *face,* because the image of my mother would mysteriously appear in my brain and I, a Big Girl Who Is Above All Things, *Nice,* just couldn't bring myself to the brink.

As Powder-Puff Girl hit bottom, the Anorexic and Big Girls Work Club heartily celebrated her demise. Despite the fact that I weighed less then than I do now, I was by no stretch of the imagination fit. But watching Powder-Puff Girl bust out of her designer duds, seeing the rolls of fat grow around her abdomen and bulge against those fitted jackets, trust me, life was *good.* Her most grotesque fashion tragedy became the infamous red Easter suit. Since it was quite possibly the only suit Powder-Puff Girl owned that she could still pour herself into, we saw it rather often. Trust me on this, red doesn't hide bulging fat *at all.*

Alas, on one particular red-Easter-suited day, we must

have laughed at Powder-Puff Girl a little too loudly while she was within earshot. Suddenly she turned, with perfect posture I might add, and headed in our direction. I swear I thought I would pee my pants, but then I remembered I had backup. I was not alone. Powder-Puff Girl stood in the doorway, thrust back her hair, and flashed her pearly whites, which might have been counted among the most classic *screw you* gestures in the Western World had there not been an enormous fleck of red lipstick on her front tooth. You can imagine the decibel level of the snickers, giggles, and guffaws in that room at the sight of Powder-Puff Girl's red tooth. No one said a word. We were so overcome with glee at her beauty faux pas, we couldn't control ourselves. As waves of hilarity rocked our bodies, Powder-Puff Girl waited patiently with a smile planted firmly on her lips and that red lipstick stuck fast. Finally we managed a modicum of self-control, and I remember someone asked, "Powder-Puff Girl *(not her real name),* can we *help* you?"

Even though Powder-Puff Girl was a relative newbie to the Big Girl World, she popped a comeback like a pro. She snarled her reply, "Oh, no. Nothing, *thanks.* Just thought you fun-loving fat gals would like to know that I'm the new sales department *manager,* that's all."

Powder-Puff Girl clicked her heels down the hallway as we members of the Anorexic and Big Girls Work Club gasped for air. Before we could utter another word, my Anorexic Friend, a petite woman who could scratch and claw the eyes right out of Abe Lincoln at Mount Rushmore, yelled, *"You've outgrown your little Easter outfit, Powder-Puff Girl! Better get mommy to take you shopping ... at a Plus-size store!"*

If you'd have looked up the phrase "hysterical apoplexy" in the dictionary, right then and there, you'd have seen us in black and white as we rolled on the floor. Anorexic Friend's insult to Powder-Puff deftly and cattily rendered Powder-Puff Girl's promotion meaningless, at least for the moment. We won the day. It was obvious that being around Big Girls had positively influenced Anorexic Friend's ability to respond to adversity through wisecracking.

I've endured my share of Big Girl insults, but none surprise me as much as those from people with whom I am well acquainted. A customer of mine in Germany, with whom I believed I enjoyed a very solid friendship, once took me to dinner at a charming castle where the restaurant was noted for its fish. I'm not much of a fish eater, although you might lay odds by the looks of me that no foodstuff on earth ever escapes my mouth uneaten, but let's just say that fish isn't among my favorite dishes *(see earlier reference to fish spaghetti)*.

After all the to-do and inane ravings of my customer about the excellence of the fish at this restaurant, I knew I had no choice but to allow him to order it for me and try to choke it down. In the belief I knew this person like the back of my hand, I expected there would be copious amounts of alcohol to accompany the fish. As every Big Girl knows, *Red Wine-slash-Beer-slash-Any Kind of Alcohol Whatsoever* is counted among the Big Girl Food Groups, so I decided I could manage to get through the evening well enough.

This incident probably ranks as the All-time Most Endless Business Dinner in the History of the World because my customer was so enthralled by the damned fish *he would not shut up!* I mean, this was a grown man, obsessed over a stupid piece of *fish!* Jonah wasn't so infatuated, I tell you. And this was the most god-awful, pungent, fishiest fish I have ever had the misfortune to know. This fish was foul, full of bones, and its little fishy head was still attached to its little fishy body *(how gross!)*.

Its beady eye glared up at me, taunting me as if to say, "Go ahead, Big Girl. Eat me, I double-dog dare ya!"

At some point in the evening, my customer stopped talking about his fish long enough to notice that my napkin was folded and I was quietly gulping my wine. He was shocked. He stared at me, then at my scarcely touched fish. I swear he turned scarlet. His face swelled up as if he might explode. At length he was able to speak. He asked soberly, "How can you *not* eat your *fish?* This is the most exquisite fish in *Deutschland,* perhaps in the *entire world,* and *you are not eating it!*"

In Germany, it is not an option to refrain from a reply. I know this because I am of German descent. Entire German provinces have wiped out each other's populations to enjoy having the last word. Silence is perceived as a challenge, such that you must goad and bait the other party into replying, so you can then have the absolute last word and win. Being the good German that my customer was, to him it was totally implausible that I had no reply to his concerns about the virtually untouched leftover fish and its cranium. He shook his head and said loudly, *"Gott in Himmel,* it can't be that you're not hungry, because *you are not a small person! You must eat all the time!* I'm sure you eat much more than this at home! How can you leave this delicacy on your plate?"

A better Big Girl than I would have said, "Excuse me, Mister Jackass Know-it-all Fish Connoisseur, I'm a grown woman. I know what I like to eat, and this ain't happenin' for me, ok? But you just keep on jammin' those little fish bones down your sorry throat and maybe I'll get lucky and you'll choke to death in about ten minutes, and then I can have

---

This being Germany, the fish would have sounded more like "Go-en zee, Bick Gurl. Eet mir, I doppel-Hund dare-en Zee, Sieg Heil!"

dessert in my room!" A better Big Girl than I would have stuck her finger down her throat and puked that exquisite fish all over my customer's plate. But I politely and silently blinked and gulped my wine, and watched as he made a total pig of himself eating not only his own fish but the remainder of mine as well. I later enjoyed a delicious main course of chocolates in my hotel room, and the next day he was so sick from all that fish eating he was late to our meeting.

Now is an excellent time to inform you of **Big Girl Secret Tip #6:** *Fish are Satan's Playthings. The words "spaghetti" and "fish" do not belong on the same line of the menu together. Never, I repeat, never, go along with a boy, even if he is the Cutest Boy in the World, on anything resembling a date where the phrase "catch our dinner" is uttered. Stay away from fish!*

Alas, as I have wasted so much of your precious time in this chapter, gentle reader, expounding upon the unpleasantness and unkindness shown to Big Girls, allow me now to lift up your spirits with a happy tale involving an act of benevolence as it was demonstrated to me. *Wow, I should write sermons, huh?*

When I gave birth to my son *(see Chapter Seven, Medical & Hormonal Issues),* he was extremely cooperative in the womb and turned himself bass-ackwards such that he was breech and, *joy unspeakable,* I skipped the whole labor and delivery thing in favor of a C-section. Some of you may question my sanity, but I was thrilled at the prospect of whipping into the hospital and whipping right out again with the baby in tow, in a few scant minutes. In any case, when it came time for my epidural, the anesthesiologist tech *(TRANSLATION: THE GUY WHO DOES ALL THE WORK BUT GETS LOUSY PAY)* was in for a long haul.

After numbing the appropriate area on my back with a local anesthetic, it was time to insert the hundred-foot long epidural tube into my spine. However in the hell they do it in the first place, I don't know, but for the pregnant woman, that would be *moi*, I had to lean over, grab my ankles with my hands, and hold my breath until the tech got that thing started in exactly the right place.

I'm not sure how many pregnant women you've encountered, but in my urgent state of Ready-to-Dropness, there was no way on God's green earth I could even think about reaching my ankles, let alone holding them and my breath simultaneously. Good grief, it had been months since I could even *see* my ankles! But, I did my best, holding my breath dutifully through several attempts while the tech sighed repeatedly. When I made a sound through my teeth resembling *"nnnnngggg,"* he said, "Ok, take a break."

I asked, "Is there a problem here?" as only a Big Girl Pregnant Woman with Attitude can ask. He was silent for a moment, then replied in a very calm voice, "Well, see, as you beautiful pregnant women know, there is a lot of extra padding back here, so it's taking me a while to get it all just right. Now, let's try again, shall we?"

I *loved* this man. I wanted to have his children. I wanted to name my baby after him and name the hospital after him and elect him President. *A beautiful woman with extra padding!* Not *FAT*, not *AN OVERABUNDANCE OF LIPIDS*, not "you're overweight" or "obese" or "how could you let yourself go, you stupid fat imbecile," but *extra padding!* This was a true humanitarian, a knight in shining armor, a warrior in the fight against … ok, you get the picture. Maybe this anesthesia tech had been smacked by one too many knocked-up, hormonal shrews to risk calling a spade a spade, but I sure remember his diplomacy. I even sent him a photo of myself with my son. As a result, he probably now lives in total seclusion at the Crazy Pregnant Patient Safehouse on the West Coast, hiding from my fanaticism. Wherever he may be, I thank him for his kindness. And now to end this chapter, it's time for **Big Girl Secret Tip #7**, courtesy of my grandmother: *Be good, be sweet, and don't eat too much meat!*

What more can I say? Lots, actually. Turn the page.

Chapter Five

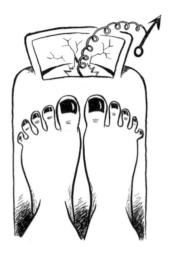

Body Image & Quick Weight Loss

Big Girls are blessed with a distinct type of vision that allows us to see ourselves as healthy, attractive, athletic, and sexy *(some would argue it isn't vision at all, it's called denial, but you can imagine what I think of <u>them</u>);* while others in our body-obsessed society might classify us as fat, lazy, repulsive, disgusting, and piggy. Therein is the problem. As my Big Girl Friend Who is Wise says, "That's why there's chocolate and vanilla." *Amen, how appropriate.*

Body image is a tough cookie to crack, for virtually every human being on earth, regardless of his or her weight, height, build, or hair color *(unless your hair is purple, and then you're most likely a Teenager with Great Angst Who Is Finding Herself, and this book is probably not for you, honey, go listen to Jewel, or weave a bracelet or something, ok?).* No matter what our size or shape or skin tone, or how attractive or unattractive we may perceive ourselves to be, is there anyone among us who truly likes her body? I have traveled extensively and talked to a lot of folks, mainly because it is impossible for me not to flap my jaws, and I have yet to meet anyone who can honestly admit they don't have a single body part or physical characteristic about themselves they wouldn't change.

Not one physical characteristic they wouldn't change ... personally, I'd trade myself in for a new model with the latest gadgets *(I already possess Side-Thigh Air Bags, thank you very much),* if I had the chance. I'm not exactly a believer in cosmetic plastic surgery as a hobby, and until they offer a convenient Full Body Exchange on every street corner, I guess I'm stuck with what I've got. I can periodically work out and try to sculpt myself and make my physique less Big-Girlish, but no matter what I do, short of cutting off a limb, it rarely sticks.

As a Big Girl, I sometimes pine for days gone by, those infamous eras where statuesque beauties romped around half-naked in Rubens' paintings and in the studios of the Renaissance masters. Even those fun-loving Impressionist painters used models with a good bit of heft to them. Modern medical experts rush to point out that the only time the Impressionists weren't intoxicated was when they stopped drinking long enough to eat their mercury-laden paints. Thus, these experts claim, such inebriated painterly depictions should not be looked on as the ideal physical representation for a healthy gal. I prefer to think that the Impressionists were simply preparing us for today's TV cameras, which add no less than ten pounds. *Don't ask me why! It's one of those things I just know. Why do you think I spent all that time and money in college, for God's sake?*

A Big Girl's image of her body typically hovers between *I'm beautiful today, hand me that éclair* or *My mother will be here in two weeks. Please help me use the vacuum to perform liposuction in the comfort of my own living room.* Body image also comes into play when our Big Girl hormones go haywire. It is not unheard of for a Big Girl to suffer from PMS and gain fourteen pounds of water in 24 hours, then take three years to shed it. An improper hormone balance can instruct our brains to go on yet another diet, particularly a diet where Quick Weight Loss is critical, as in, *I'll button these damned jeans if it kills me, Mister Right's at the door!* Here is **Big Girl Secret Tip #8:** *Never begin any Quick Weight Loss diet that requires you to surgically remove your internal organs, sever a limb, or alter your conscious state in a manner alien to your particular life form.*

Let's review: A Big Girl, let's call her Daisy, wakes up one morning after a less-than-stellar sexual experience with her husband, wherein he nicknamed each of her love handles before promptly falling asleep and ignoring her personal satisfaction. Daisy decides here and now to lose 100 pounds in six to eight weeks, a reasonably attainable goal in her opinion, in order to borrow her daughter's slinky, black velvet dress, wear it to her 25th high school reunion, and have a Secret Sexual Tryst with her ex-boyfriend, Mister Ever-ready. She knows for a fact Mister Ever-ready still has a thing for her, because *a)* he lives across the country and has no idea she's now the size of Rhode Island, *b)* the photo she so recently e-mailed him featured her head on her slim friend Mary's body, and *c)* his suggestive reply bordered on the obscene. Daisy is determined to drop 100 pounds *fast,* and she begins to chant the American Weight Loss Mantra, *Do Whatever It Takes.* This, my friends, is dieting desperation, but it happens day in and day out across our country. Let's not be faint of heart, but press on.

Daisy packs herself up and heads for the bookstore, where she is confronted with no fewer than 3,500 titles involving weight loss and proper nutrition. After forty-two years of attempted weight loss, she's seen them all: the Cabbage Diet, the Hard-Boiled Egg Diet, the Low-Carb Diet, the No-Carb Diet, and the controversial No Food Whatsoever Diet. Daisy spies a new title of interest, *WEIGHT LOSS THROUGH SEVERE DIARRHEA,* but none of these books specifically address Daisy's need to lose roughly half her body weight in less than 60 days, so you can surely understand her frustration. Daisy staggers out of the bookstore, on the verge of tears, when she spots a flyer on a telephone pole. She moves closer, lifts up her bifocals in order to read the small print, and makes a note of the phone number. She returns to her car, locks the door, and nervously dials the number using her cell phone.

Daisy is instructed by a very smooth voice to drive three blocks to the river, walk across a ramp to a rusty barge, and come in for a Free Assessment, which she does. As she enters the Foolproof American Therapeutic Substance Organization Weight Loss Center *(FATSO, for short),* Daisy already feels ten pounds lighter. The rusty exterior belies the very definition of spa luxury in the barge's inner sanctum. Everywhere Daisy looks there are Big Girls like herself, running around in thick Turkish towels and little pink spa sandals. A wonderful aroma *(no, it can't be ... brownies?)* wafts through the air, combined with another, indescribable scent, perhaps a strange combination of burning sugar and shrubbery. Daisy relaxes. *This is it, she thinks, this time, I can do it!* She steps up to a very tanned, very toned, very together woman at the counter, whose pupils are the size of melons, and informs the woman of her wish to lose 100 pounds in six to eight weeks. *"What an excellent goal-maker you are,"* the woman says calmly. *"Someone with such a fire under her ass will have absolutely no trouble losing weight at FATSO, believe me! Now, read this booklet. It's our liability statement. No big deal. Fill out these patient forms in triplicate. See me when you're finished. My name is LaTonia."* Of course it is.

Daisy sits down in a cushy, pink chair *(is this butter-smooth leather or what?)* and begins to read the liability statement, which is roughly the size of the Gutenberg Bible. She begins to lose interest in the liability statement at the sight of so many cheerful women in towels, chatting and sipping bottled water, and *yes, they are eating brownies! This is a program I can live with.* Daisy picks up the patient forms and clicks open her pen, wondering if LaTonia neglected to give her the FATSO fee schedule. *No matter,* Daisy thinks to herself, *money is no object. Let's get down to it,* and she does.

In the interest of time, Big Girls, since you may have cookies or a pie, or both, in the oven, here are the first few questions on Daisy's patient form:

1) *Have you ever, to your knowledge, participated in any medical program where a technically illegal substance was administered on a floating barge?*

2) *Do you fully comprehend the meaning behind the name of the famous rock group, the Doobie Brothers?*

3) *Would you describe your personality as addictive, and if so, have you ever received treatment for this addiction, or worse, been incarcerated?*

4) *If you answer yes to any of the following, please see your Client Satisfaction Associate immediately before proceeding:*
   a) *Do you have a federal prison record?*
   b) *Are you on parole or wearing an in-house arrest bracelet?*
   c) *Do you have a personal relationship with Manuel Noriega? (May we contact you at a confidential number?)*
   d) *Are you a member of any Witness Protection Organization?*
   e) *Are you employed by any local, state, or federal governmental agency?*

f) *Are you presently packing a firearm?*

g) *Is your current annual household income less than $100,000?*

h) *Do you presently have, on retainer, a good defense attorney?*

i) *Are you currently undergoing any type of radical treatment for the improvement of glaucoma?*

j) *Are you under surveillance, or did anyone follow you here?*

At this point in the process, Daisy is now thoroughly confused. She has no idea how these ridiculous questions have anything whatsoever to do with dramatic weight loss results. However, when another cadre of giggling, brownie-munching, towel-wrapped women passes her chair, Daisy overlooks her frustration, and continues:

5) *Would you describe your need to lose weight as (select one):*
   a) *Looking for a Party*
   b) *Committed*
   c) *Desperate*
   d) *Life-threatening*
   e) *Imperative to my ability to pack myself into a taxi and get home*

6) *Would you describe your body type as (select one):*
   a) *Pear-shaped*
   b) *Apple-shaped*
   c) *Cone-shaped*
   d) *Orca the Whale*
   e) *The Michelin Man*
   f) *Butterball*
   g) *I'm just here with my pusher*

7) *To what lengths would you go to achieve your personal weight loss goals and pay for this service should your financial situation become problematic?*

 a) *Hock my extremely large diamond(s)*

 b) *Hock my expensive foreign car(s)*

 c) *Cash in on my husband's life insurance policy (no specific details, <u>please</u>)*

 d) *Sign over my Swiss bank account(s)*

 e) *Make FATSO my legal heir*

8) *Certain patients may qualify for our Foreign Treatment program, with free trips to Mexico and back on occasion, all expenses paid. To be eligible, you must not be under a current extradition order, and you must be physically able to swim across a deep channel or run approximately one mile into a desert gorge in under four minutes. The possession of a passport is optional. Welcome!*

At this point, Daisy is utterly confounded. The *"describe your body type"* question has given her a headache. How could she possibly guess the correct answer? She is now uncertain as to whether she can complete the patient forms in time to meet her girlfriends for lunch at New Deli. She moves to the counter, and LaTonia hands her a fee schedule. Daisy silently reads the fees, which for your convenience, are printed here:

FATSO Weight Loss Center Membership Fees

One session per week (includes all treatment substances) *$200*

Two sessions per week (plus extra brownies) *$350*

Three sessions per week (and a pack of papers) *$500*

Customized Personal Program** . . . . . ***Current street price*

Daisy is *shocked.* She cannot possibly pay this kind of money over the course of six to eight weeks, especially when she doesn't know a single soul who can attest to this program's results! *What are they using on these women?* she wonders. *It must be some super cellulite cream!* Daisy hands the incomplete forms to LaTonia, who scowls. Daisy nervously stutters, "I'm sorry, but I ... I ... I have an appointment to ... to ... take my expensive foreign car in for servicing and pick up my extremely large diamonds at the jeweler's this afternoon, and I'm afraid I've run out of time. *Thank you so much!*"

Daisy exits the FATSO parking lot, where no less than ten women in late-model convertible sports cars are anxiously waiting for her parking space. As she drives home, Daisy quickly calculates the amount of time left before her high school reunion, and decides that a ten-pound weight loss would be much more achievable, if not healthier for her body. She whips back into the bookstore, purchases a slim volume entitled, *YOUR WIFE'S SEXUAL SATISFACTION FOR NITWITS,* and drives home with the knowledge that her love handles will soon be put to good use, nickname or no. After another taxing mental calculation, Daisy realizes that her husband should be able to complete his new sexual study guide in the proverbial six to eight weeks, and this brings a smile to her face. She may have to pass on attending that high school reunion, but at least her anticipated Wild Weekend of Love will yet come to pass, in the comfort of her own home, and she won't have to worry about catching crabs from Mister Everready. She steals a glimpse of her body in the hall mirror and thinks to herself, *This outfit is so slimming. I believe it's time for a Goo-Goo Cluster®!*

Daisy is not alone in her Diet Frustration. Virtually every Big Girl has endured countless road trips down the Diet

Highway, and it usually ain't pretty. There are Bible-based diets, various and sundry "factor" diets, The Absolute Last Diet, Carb Busters, Butt Busters, Peanut Buster Parfaits® *(oops, sorry, that's at Dairy Queen),* and a host of weight-reduction programs out there for the choosing. I'm living proof that some of them actually work. I can say without a doubt that I've lost about three thousand pounds with their help, over the course of thirty-five years. And now it's so easy ... no more foodstuff measuring angst, you simply bebop over to the grocery store, fill your cart with pre-packaged Diet Program Food, eat it, and total up your points.

The problem with any diet program is that Big Girls are skeptics. *Yes, Madame Instructor, I listened when you told me I couldn't possibly inhale two pounds of chocolate a day on the program and still lose weight. But I have to see for myself!* Nobody tells a Big Girl what to do! It has to be *my decision* not to eat the chocolate, and that will happen precisely when Pigs Fly Around the Earth Handing Out Tacos. My idea of a successful diet program would be to handcuff myself to a refrigerator that only contained carrots, celery, and bottled water. But, being the Resourceful Big Girl that I am, I'd probably do a "McGyver" and use my toenail clippings to pick the lock on the handcuff, and that would be it. House-arrest bracelets might work on a few Big Girls, but I'd just pay a homeless person to do my secret shopping and use my Fail-Safe Food Hiding Places. These creative options are not presently available in my demographic area, however, so when it's time to diet, I sign up and start the program, major motivated. I might even lose a few pounds, but then I begin to slide. *That cookie is calling my name from the pantry, I swear. SHUT UP COOKIE!* Then I quickly roll downhill at a very fast Large Round Object pace.

Let's review a sinister, potentially life-threatening humanoid, that of the Weight Loss Program Administrator. You know the drill ... pay a lot of money, go to a weekly meeting, and try not to burst into hysterical belly laughs at the "sharing" wherein a bunch of overweight folks tell themselves that a diet of carrot curls and gravel can indeed lead to Ultimate Earthly Joy. Typically when you approach the Weigh-In Room, there are lots of curtained booths from which to choose. You're supposed to enter one of these booths, under the supervision of the Weight Loss Administrator, or as I fondly call her, Satan's Accursed Handmaiden, and weigh yourself, God forbid, *with your shoes on.* This is completely ludicrous, because then the Accursed Handmaiden, after sneering and saying something like, *"Oh, I see we didn't adhere to Our Program very well this week, did we?"* rudely informs you that she will now deduct a couple pounds from the weight on the scale to account for your shoes. If she could have simply allowed me to remove my shoes in the first place, there wouldn't be a need for all this cooking the books now, would there? And who made her the World's Arbiter of Shoe Weight in the first place?

One summer, my Big Girl Diet Expert Friend and I joined one of these programs. We did not like the attitude of our particular Accursed Handmaiden *at all.* She droned on for ten minutes about the life-threatening penalties we would incur without rigid adherence to the Program Card Filing System. She added the phrase "don't we" to everything she said. I quote: *"We all love our veggies, don't we? We drink four hundred gallons of water every day, don't we? We all know what will happen if we don't file our cards properly, don't we?" "We all know what a bitch the Program Administrator is, don't we?"* Oh, no, sorry. I made that up.

My Big Girl Diet Expert Friend and I actually worked the program, for once, and according to our home scales, we lost weight. So you can imagine our frustration when the Accursed Handmaiden from Hell informed us at Weigh-In that we had each gained a pound. We demanded an explanation. We requested a re-weigh on another scale, to which the Accursed Handmaiden from Hell replied, "These scales are professionally calibrated to within one-quarter of one ounce. I suggest you go home and re-examine your commitment to this lifestyle."

Yeah, well these fists are professionally calibrated to sock you in the face if you don't let me take off my shoes! We devised a Plan. We informed the Accursed Handmaiden that due to a prior engagement, we needed to exit the "sharing" part of the meeting early, and she nodded her understanding. After enduring the "sharing" of two classmates, including one unbelievable tale of inexplicable horror surrounding the actual choice of an apple over a slice of pie, my Big Girl Diet Expert Friend and I waved our goodbyes, and slipped from the room. We promptly removed our shoes, stepped on the scale in each of the little booths and compared notes. I have no doubt those scales were professionally calibrated all right ... just not to any measurement that any human being invented or can comprehend. Let me tell you, those scales were Instruments of the Devil. To say they were inaccurate is to say that the Grand Canyon is a little ditch.

Next we weighed our shoes and, no surprise here, with our Big Girl feet, they were no less than *three* pounds a pair ... the Accursed Handmaiden from Hell was *preventing* us from achieving our weight loss goals, it was a *set-up!* We right then and there tore up our Program Cards and threw them on the floor. In a split-second of inspiration that was divined on the behalf of Big Girls everywhere, we stared at the rows of

Program Cards neatly filed in long boxes on a table. I looked at my Big Girl Diet Expert Friend, and we both smiled. Quick as a wink, we grabbed handfuls of those Program Cards and mixed the A's with the W's and the B's with the K's. You get the picture. The Accursed Handmaiden from Hell no doubt suffered an apoplectic fit and is most likely now living in a sanitorium. We skipped to our car and rewarded ourselves for our gumption with a trip to the Krispy Kreme drive-thru. What a red-letter day! But I digress … too bad, it's my book and I can digress whenever the heck I want to.

Here are a few lame reasons **Why Big Girls Should Join a Weight Loss Program** (included only because my Editor threatened to withhold my chocolate if I didn't):

1) *You must attend meetings, where you are held accountable.* Attending a meeting on your least favorite subject, the withholding of food, is not what any sensible Big Girl wants to do on her own time. But if you must go, then lie to your boss and attend during work hours. Then stop and get a snack afterwards, because Lord knows you'll need it.

2) *You won't believe the number of low-fat recipes you'll receive that use Cool Whip®.* I think it's in direct response to the Big Girl "Gravy as a Vegetable" concept, but there are plenty of recipes for things like "Pineapple Fluff" and "Strawberry Fluff" and other items in the Fluff category. If you are one of those people who thinks a new tub of Cool Whip is better than Christmas morning, knock yourself out.

3) *You get cool Diet Toys.* Most Big Girls are obsessive-compulsive, to the point of excess, and this is true even in our

Dieting Mode. If we are serious about a Diet, we know it like the back of our hand. We've typed it up on our computer and distributed it to friends. We play with our Diet Toys: Charts, Counters, Books, and Food Journals to the point of driving our friends insane. But *let's review* for a sec about Food Journals, ok? If I were to write down, in complete and total honesty, everything I ate in a week and put it in a Food Journal, the volume of paper required would exceed that of the current tort filings in our country as we speak. Speaking of tortes ... *mmm, Black Forest torte,* how many points is that?

4) *There are bigger Big Girls than you on the program.* Oh, I'm going to burn in hell for this little confession, but if you're gonna be a bear, be a grizzly. Don't you love to attend a weight loss program meeting and behave like a Thin Person, comparing yourself to the others in the room, and thinking, *At least I'm not as big as her! How could she let herself go like that, she has such a pretty face?*

Chapter Six

Clothes, Makeup, Hair & Its Removal

Until corsets and bustles burst on the scene, Big Girls the world over enjoyed a Fashion Free For All, in that *haute couture* consisted mainly of your garden-variety peasant gunnysack, the big-as-a-house muslin shift *(an ancient forerunner of the modern muu muu),* or your classic toga and cape ensemble. Undergarments were optional in those barbaric times, but at least you didn't have to worry about a slenderizing profile or whether your Big Girl Abdominal Assets would pop the buttons right off your pants in the middle of an important meeting.

Today we have The Really Big Secret lingerie catalogue, where, in the privacy of our own homes, we can order slinky Big Girl lingerie over the telephone and toy with the customer service rep *(yes,* I did just say *52DD,* and wouldn't *you* like to see those babies!)* fully aware that the person on the other end will never know what we look like in such a naughty contraption.

Now let's share another **Big Girl Universal Truism guaranteed to save you lots of time so you can stop and have a hot fudge sundae while shopping:** *There is absolutely no need to ever, ever try on lingerie to determine how it will look on your person. Just take the lingerie you covet and throw it on the floor, because that's where it's gonna end up anyway, ladies.* Chances are, if it looks great on the floor, it will do the trick, unless it's football season.

Big Girl clothing has come a long way since my childhood. Then, if I wanted to wear anything besides blue jeans, the options available to "chubbies" or the truly rude version, "chubbettes," were made from polyester imprinted with huge, brightly colored flowers. Sporting these less-than-fashionable garments with my short haircut, I pretty much resembled Don Ho for several years. All that's changed now. No more wearing the draperies or granny's tablecloth for Big Girls, no ma'am! But, revert back with me a sec, to the subject of *not* trying on lingerie. ***Let's review:*** Why is it that when there are so many mirrored dressing rooms in this mall-crazed country of ours, Big Girls insist on wearing clothes that don't fit?

Here is the **Ultimate Big Girl List of Fashion No-Nos.** I beg you, take note.

1) *Anything featuring horizontal stripes.* Double Wides R Us. *Not.*

2) *Red-sequined hot pants with black, fishnet stockings.* Steer

clear of this wardrobe selection, please. Keywords to avoid are "hot" and "fishnet."

3) **Belly shirts.** Big Girl bare navels are not the wildly exciting stimulus you believe them to be, ok?

4) **Tube tops.** The entire world is not your Daytona Race Day infield. *Please* don't show us your tits, unless you're at Mardi Gras, a hooker, or both.

5) **Sleeveless shirts.** This is a toughie. Lord knows I'd never send a Big Girl out into the bloodthirsty world of fashion without a manual, so pay attention. I have a Tiny Girl Friend Who Has Big Arms *(don't ask)*. Her husband has been known, on occasion, to poke at the flab under the backs of her arms and remark "BOK, BOK." His explanation for this seemingly idiotic behavior is that this attribute of his beloved reminds him of the skin under the neck of a chicken, in the best way possible. *So.* Check your "BOK, BOK" quotient before going sleeveless, that's all I ask.

6) **Skin-tight jeans.** Here's the test: if you have to hang from a chandelier in order to get yourself into these puppies, punt.

7) **Flowered muu muus or any selection from the muu muu family.** 'Nuf said.

8) **Leather miniskirts with matching halter tops and stiletto heels.** Ditto.

9) **See-through gauzy items paired with zebra print underwear.** Double ditto.

10) *A full-body catsuit with gold lamé shoes.* Lordy be, it's Big
    Fat Catgirl!

There is one last **Fashion No-No,** but it's a tad on the
touchy side and truly out of our hands to control. It's the
Dreaded Big Girl Bridesmaid Dress. If your absolute Best Friend
on Earth is getting hitched, and invites you to stand by her side
at the ceremony, you really can't refuse, unless you can some-
how contract smallpox and be quarantined for several months.
Any female of the girl persuasion knows that the secret to a
beautiful wedding is to find the most gruesome bridesmaid
dresses in the world and force your best friends to wear them in
public, for several hours, in front of everyone you know.

The reason for this behavior is to allow the Bride to believe
that she is, for one day, the Most Beautiful Girl in the World,
and can point to her bridesmaids and proudly say, *"See my
friends, don't they look hideous? They're my very best friends in the
world, and they all look so ugly, don't they? And I look soooo
gooood."* This time-honored tradition ain't gonna stop just
because you are a Big Girl. No, ma'am. When your Best Friend
on Earth shows you a delightful sleeveless selection in seafoam
green, with a fitted bodice, full skirt, and a flouncy ruffle on
your derrière, you have to stand and take your punishment,
and remember that when it's your turn, revenge will be oh-so-
sweet. God forbid the bridesmaid gifts consist of cute little
necklaces, because you won't be able to fit them around your
Big Girl neck. You can always get out of this at the last minute
with, *"Oh, shit! I can't believe I left that necklace at home and it's
only three minutes until the wedding!"*

Thankfully Big Girls can now simply walk into their
favorite discount store and buy clothes in their size, *right off the
rack. Hallelujah!* But there are retail limits, darling. No self-

respecting Big Girl would ever be caught dead in a store with the name "Dress Barn." *All you heifers line up, rightchere, an' gitcha some new feedsacks!* Modern apparel purveyors have discovered that they can lease a gigantic retail space, slap one name on the front, and divide the store into two discreet sections: Clothes for Thin Girls and Clothes for Attractive, Beautiful Big Girls. These people obviously paid attention in Marketing 101, and thank God for them. In any clothing store where Big Girl Apparel is sold, you must select carefully, however, because some of this stuff is made in China, India, or Bangladesh, where they really don't understand the concept of a size 3X. Just make sure you try before you buy and you'll be fine.

Here is the **Ultimate Big Girl List of 10 Fashion Must-Haves:**

1) *Plus-Sized Knee-Hi's.* Honey, buy your dresses long and throw out those full-sized panty hose. No more crotch-rippin' for you! Knee-hi's are where it's at, trust me on this. And for winter wear, trouser socks work just as well as knee-hi's. But purchase the Big Girls' sizes. The Phyllis Diller Roll-Down look is so *passé.*

2) *The Big Girl Big Shirt.* This is essential. One can never own too many, because we need them in every color. And the whole straight hem or shirt-tail argument is silly ... when do Big Girls with any ounce of Intelligence *ever* tuck in their shirts? Buy them at least 33" long to cover your hoo-ha hiney and pair them with leggings *(see below)*. And, no synthetic fabrics, ladies. Nothing is as cling-free and forgiving as pure, unadulterated cotton.

3) *A Lands' End® Big Girl Swimsuit.* I *love* the people at Lands' End. The first time my Lands' End catalog arrived touting "NEW WOMEN'S SIZES" I dropped the chocolate cake I was eating, fell down on the floor of my kitchen, and sobbed tears of joy. Kudos to the first major clothing manufacturer to use actual Big Girls to design and model swimsuits and other items, and for making the first Big Girl swimsuit that won't stretch out or fall apart at the seams or fade after you wear it twice! After you pick out a cute suit, get yourself a cover-up and a little straw hat. You'll be struttin' like the Big Girl from Ipanema!

4) *Leggings and Stretch Pants.* In grade school we used to call these "leotards," but true leggings are more opaque. The beauty of leggings is first and foremost their ability to stretch over your Big Girl legs. When paired with a Big Girl Shirt *(see above)* that hangs down to the knees, well, it's such a cute look, I just can't begin to describe it on paper.

5) *Proper Undergarments.* What I am about to say may cause a veritable underwear riot, but it must be said. *THROW OUT THOSE GRANNY PANTS!* And please, get rid of the Days of the Week Polyester specials, ok? Just because you are a Big Girl doesn't mean you can't have Sexy Undies like your Thin friends! The Jockey® folks are on the Clue Bus. They offer Big Girl sizes in the most absolutely fabulous undies on earth, the French Cut Cotton Panty. Let's face it, as a Big Girl you already have lots of extra things happening around your mid-section. Why would you want a great big handful of cotton granny underwear in there also, to bunch up when you sit down? These Jockey

French Cuts are the way to go. Trust me on this.

6) ***Spandex Anything.*** Shorts, shirts, pants, socks ... I just can't live life as a Big Girl without spandex. My favorite article is a black spandex and cotton dress that rolls up like a ball but never wrinkles. I look like a million bucks when I wear this to a party paired with a Big Girl Big Shirt. *Thank you, God, for spandex. Amen.*

7) ***Linen Pantsuits.*** Linen is the fabric of the rich and famous, and Big Girls. It doesn't cling. It is always the height of timeless fashion. When you drop your iced tea in your lap, it dries quickly. Junonia catalogs have great linen pantsuits, among other things. Check them out. Liz and Jane® Clothes, those veritable linen experts based in Panama City Beach, Florida, make linen clothes *to die for.* Liz and Jane is my signature clothing line as a Famous Author (TRANSLATION: FREE HANDOUTS WOULD BE APPRECIATED).

8) ***Ray-Ban® Sunglasses.*** There's something about a Big Girl in Hip Sunglasses that makes us stand out from the crowd, despite our being head and shoulders taller and outweighing the average citizen by say, forty percent. Big Girls, use your God-given right to look *cool!*

9) ***A Black Cardigan.*** All Big Girls worth their hot fudge know the Power of Black. With a black cardigan sweater, you can take over the world. Headed to the movies with a bunch of Big Girl Friends in jeans? Toss a black cardigan around your shoulders and you'll be the One He Notices, as in He Who Pours the Butter on the Popcorn. Business

trip to Chicago? Slap a black cardigan over your dress, pop on those Ray-Bans, and head to Oprah's studio, baby. You're lookin' *good*.

10) *Last but not least, the Frumpy At-Home Outfit.* There are some days Big Girls just don't wanna truck with nobody. You want to stay in, catch up on your reading, and there's a three-gallon vat of Chocolate Chocolate Chip in the freezer calling your name. For these festive occasions I recommend a classy combination of gray, worn-out sweatpants topped with a green, knee-length cotton nightgown. Of course I would never presume to foist my style upon you. Be forewarned: I rarely answer the door when I am attired in this fashion. There are spies from the top Paris clothing designers camped in my yard, day in, day out, scopin' me out like Jackie O.

Now ladies, commit this list to your respective Big Girl memories and go shopping. And don't forget to stop for a snack, lunch, and dessert. I mean, really, who would expect you to carry around all those heavy bags without fortification? Let's move now to the subject of our pretty faces, shall we?

The application of makeup, for some women, is a competitive sport. I personally have never been too interested in makeup: they could solve the oil problem in this country by tapping my face, so the idea of coating my cheeks with a substance containing significant amounts of petroleum doesn't sound like a very good idea *pour moi*. Don't get me wrong. I wore the requisite blue eye shadow in seventh grade, clear up to my forehead like all the girls, in my role as Big Girl Love Advisor. But the one time in my life when I did use all of the makeup products in my possession, in exactly the order and amount that they were prescribed, my own family didn't recognize me and a close friend asked if I was trying to conceal a serious illness.

It now seems appropriate to address the situation of perspiration, another reason why this particular Big Girl refrains from wearing much makeup. My mother always told me that nice girls *(in my case, Nice Big Girls)* don't sweat, they "glow." *God bless our Big Girl mothers* ... they were in worse denial than we ever realized, weren't they? Oh well, they had to survive the Fifties, and that wreaked havoc with almost everyone's sanity. But let me tell you, after I've hauled three twelve-packs of imported beer and a bag of chips into the house, "glow" is not a word that adequately describes my physical condition. I do love my mom, however, so in the interest of familial relationships, I continue to say *"I'm glowing."* I regularly red-line the glow meter right up there with Area 51, except that Area 51's makeup probably stays put, with all the low humidity inherent in the New Mexican desert.

Certain Big Girls among us have the Art of Deceptive Makeup down pat. Give these kids a fishing tackle box full of creams, rouges, powders, and paints and they can make themselves look a good five pounds thinner in only three hours! It's a pretty good trick, too, considering they've actually added twelve pounds of makeup to their visage. We're talkin' *professionals,* here.

Once my Big Girl Friend Who is Fashionable and I went to a fancy department store and headed straight for the expensive makeup section. Did you know that those five or six tony brands are all owned by the same company and that it's all the same stuff in different packaging? Anyhow, my girlfriend and I decided that if we didn't get makeovers right then and there, we would shrivel up and die. Big Girls don't shrivel well. It is not a pretty sight.

We approached one of the counters where the female clerks resemble ex-supermodels and beauty queens, except that they wear lab coats to impart the impression that they are Makeup Scientific Geniuses. *Right.* We informed one of the clerks that we both wanted to be made-over. If you could have, right then and there, looked up "deer-in-the-headlights," you'd have seen this gal's picture. We plopped our Big Girl hineys down into those tiny little chairs that are made for cartoon stick figures, and we winked at each other. *This is gonna be good!*

To say that we created quite a stir is an understatement of vast proportion. Not only did we demand makeovers, we insisted on sampling every single shade of every product on their well-stocked shelves. There was so much lipstick and eye-liner on the backs of our hands and arms, we looked like walking bar codes. After we'd pretty much exhausted the reservoir of makeup samples, my Big Girl Friend Who is Fashionable inquired, "Don't you sell anything that gives the illusion of slimness?"

Oh, for a camera to record for posterity the look on Miss Deer-in-the-Headlights' face! It was obvious that her extensive makeup training had not included How to Deal with Snotty Big Girls With Time on Their Hands, and for a split second, we thought she would cry.

I want you to know, that clerk didn't skip a beat. She pointed one glamorous, well-manicured finger, and said, "Yes, I think we do have something … it's in our new product line, just a minute." Dumbstruck, we waited silently until the clerk returned with what appeared to be a large paper bag. My friend was about to come to blows with this skinny gal, thinking she was gonna put this bag over our heads, until she realized that the woman did indeed have a product up her veritable sleeve.

From this large paper bag the clerk retrieved something called a "Shadow Stick," which is used around your jaw line, to, *guess what,* create the illusion of slimness! Of course, if you actually use it, as we later learned, there's no illusion of slimness at all … the illusion is that you work at the circus and have forgotten to remove the pancake makeup from your neck, or that you are a homeless person who has refrained from bathing for several weeks and now sport a permanent brown crust under your chin.

How do we know? Because we both bought that Shadow Stick, and one of every other product this clever clerk brought out and demonstrated to us, for the purposes of creating illusions of slimness on assorted parts of our bodies. She might not have been a Makeup Scientific Genius, but I'd lay odds that this gal made an "*A*" in Salesmanship, because she filled up that large paper bag with every item we purchased, as quickly as you can say MasterCard®. I may not wear much makeup, but honey, that doesn't mean I don't own a truckload. I can use it any time I want to, as long as I'm not glowing.

So here's *Big Girl Secret Tip #9: Follow the makeup tips of the European women, who are oh-so-elegant. Simply wear a little eyeliner (no raccoon eyes, please), a little lipstick, drink lots of water and get plenty of fresh air to make your cheeks look flushed. If you think you need something more, tie a silk scarf around your neck and hold your head high.* Man, this is really a legitimate whoop-ass tip, isn't it? Well, it works! I've seen it in action, so hush.

Last on our all-inclusive list of important beauty topics is *Hair & Its Removal.* Since we're in the *H* section, we may as well talk about the Hair that is on our Heads for a moment. Well, maybe it's on *your* head … I learned, after giving birth to my son, that after nine months of properly nourishing his every need, he had sufficiently drained every ounce of thyroid hormone from my body. My hair fell out in clumps. It is my only physical feature that could ever, in your wildest imagination, be described as thin. Don't get me started ...

Hair for modern Big Girls has mainly consisted of three styles designed to draw attention away from our midsections and up toward our heads: braids *á la* Brunhilde, or its most recent adaptation, the Retro-Hippie-Earth Mother look; the Big Girl Bouffant *(otherwise known as 1950s Southern Belle Hair);* or the Pixie. My mother always favored the Pixie "because it accentuates your pretty face." Yeah, let's skip that old dumpy body and cut right to the cute do, shall we? My hair was routinely cut so short I could have passed for a boy or a POW. My face was accentuated all over the place, let me tell you. To this day, I don't feel as if I've received the ultimate haircut value if my ears don't show and my neck isn't shaved.

Once my mom, in a wild episode of uncharacteristic frivolity, allowed me to do the Southern Belle thing, complete with a large, red bow lacquered right into the middle of my scalp. I swear the hairdresser used at least one full can of White Rain® to hold that do in poufy position. Every morning before school, my mom topped off the hairspray a tad more, so that by the end of the week I resembled what was later interpreted as the lady Conehead on "Saturday Night Live." I remembered that my scalp itched continuously, and the red bow was a curious object with a life of its own. It would pop off for no apparent reason, usually in the middle of fifth-grade choir, forcing the teacher to scowl and raise her arm for us to stop singing "Strangers in the Night" so I might retrieve my errant hair accessory and get back to business.

I swiftly returned to the Pixie out of desperation, though I suffered ghost pains where my bouffant used to be. For three days I couldn't move my head independent of my body. Herein lies **Big Girl Secret Tip #10:** *Skip the bouffant, honey. Throw out the hairspray before that giant rat's nest you so fondly call your hair gives birth to some unidentifiable species of alien and takes over our planet. Get yourself a Pixie and be done with it. If you get bored with short hair, change the color every six weeks … it'll really mess with your husband's mind and you'll endear your hairdresser.*

Because I'm jealous as a hornet, this is quite enough talk about hair, thank you, since I don't have much. Now, let's turn to the subject of Hair Removal, and really have some fun, ok? I can prove that God has a sense of humor, because while the hair on my head is falling out, the hair on my face and neck is growing thicker and darker, *like a man's!* After I recently spent half the day in front of the bathroom mirror in various and sundry states of plucking and tweezing, I decided to go to the proverbial Mountain of Big Girl Advice. I called my Big Girl Friend Who Obsesses Over Hair Removal to discuss this bodily phenomenon, and after she quoted me chapter and verse about the fact that I was most likely undergoing peri-menopause *(see Chapter Seven, Medical & Hormonal Issues),* we got down to brass tacks. I drove to her house, entered her bathroom, and viewed on display no less than 47 products designed to remove all traces of hair from a Big Girl's body. In fact, my friend and her husband have a competition going: every time he buys a new fly rod or similar fishing accoutrement, she spends an equivalent amount on the latest hair removal product. *It is a sickness …*

Fortunately for you, I will share the benefits of the endless laboratory tests I endured in this chick's bathroom. Here follows the **Ultimate Big Girl Consumer Test Results on Hair Removal Products:**

1) *Tweezing:* This is perhaps the easiest and least expensive option, short of doing nothing and being confused with the Bearded Lady. Tweezing is best performed after moistening the area to be treated with a warm washcloth, and after swallowing five Top-Shelf margaritas, with salt. The problem with tweezing is not, surprisingly, the pain, but the fact that you can become cross-eyed trying to pluck your eyebrows, which simply is not a good look for a Big Girl *at all.*

2) *Waxing:* A timeless method of hair removal that was invented by the Spanish Inquisition, waxing not only removes unwanted hair and renders the affected skin baby-smooth, it offers the risk of second-degree burns and muscle spasms as you twitch in fear of the approaching beautician. How fun is that? Did you know that in Los Angeles, Wax Technicians to the Stars create little designs with wax in the hair on one's *tootie?* No, I didn't think you knew that. *Yuuuuck ...*

3) *Shaving:* Every Big Girl worth her Burma-Shave® knows that razors are fine for removing hair from appendages, and ... *hey, get your minds out of the gutter!* It is the strict medical opinion of the *Big Girl's Guide to Life* staff that shaving is not at all recommended for eyebrows *(don't laugh, we tried it);* the lip line *(unless you're a Man, and then shame on you for reading this book);* or the bikini area, unless you want to do the Bowlegged Cowboy Saunter *(see Exercise & Its Avoidance)* due to the resulting irritation.

4) *Hair Removal Cream:* Possibly the simplest method we shall discuss, simply slather the cream on your legs, then

stand in the bathtub until either your hair or skin comes off in tiny pieces. Collect the large pieces of skin in a moist cloth and drive yourself, with your epidermis collection in tow, to the nearest Skin Graft Center.

5) *The All-Natural, Green, Rip-off-the-Skin-with-your-Hair Gel:* You've seen the TV infomercial, you've seen it in drugstores, perhaps you've even purchased it but are deathly afraid to use it. Trust me on this … *don't,* unless you enjoy having large strips of yourself pulled from your body without the benefit of morphine or other narcotics. Aloe vera smoothing lotion gives instant relief, *my ass! (see Skin Graft Center, above)*

6) *The Pull-the-Hair-Out-by-the-Root Machine:* A favorite of men who shop at midnight on Christmas Eve, this little torture device should not be sold without a license to perform surgery. It is interesting, however, to measure exactly how long those ol' roots can be.

7) *Electrolysis:* Here is what it feels like to undergo electrolysis, Big Girl … put your finger into an electrical socket until you jump at least three feet into the air from the pain, repeatedly, for about two hours. Need I say more?

8) *The Fuzz-B-Gone System:* These gems must have been invented by a man with an axe to grind. There's a strip that looks very much like a piece of 60-grit sandpaper that you rub over the desired area until you sustain a first-degree burn, and the heat from the resulting fire singes the hair from your person. Makes an ideal gift for a man with a hairy back, especially if you're trying to dump him. Whip this

sucker out, use it, and trust me, he'll be over you by the time you can say, "Oh, did that *hurt?*" Ditto for the mitt, which you are supposed to *"gently rub on your face in light, circular motions until hair disappears."* After using this method, my friends believed I'd had a kinky rendezvous because my cheeks sported what appeared to be rug burn.

9) *The Ancient Art of Middle Eastern Silk Thread Hair Removal:* I have no idea how this works, and am deathly afraid to try it, despite the fact that I have a non-Big Girl Friend from Iran who offered to teach me and another Hairy American Big Girl the time-honored secrets of the thread removal system. Ya know, if it does the trick, and I mean no disrespect here, why do all the women in that part of the world go around with their faces covered? Sounds like false advertising to me. Plus, next to every woman hiding behind a veil is a Really Large Guy with a Machete, so I'm challenging you, gentle reader, to boldly go where no Big Girl has gone before with this thread thing, and then call me.

Big Girls of the World, we have now presented you with enough knowledge of Hair Removal to make an informed decision regarding the purchase of said products and the use of said technologies. Me, I'm off to the circus. That Bearded Lady gig doesn't sound so bad … it comes with all the popcorn and cotton candy you can eat.

Chapter Seven

Medical & Hormonal Issues

Today's medical society prides itself in extolling the virtues of a low-fat, low-cholesterol, low-fun lifestyle. I guess if I spent roughly ten years of my life in med school treating street people and patients who practice personal hygiene on a bi-annual basis, I, too, might be predisposed to take out my revenge on the entire population and convince them that they should eat nothing but oat bran and tofu, once I sported a Doctor name tag on my lapel.

Have you ever been to a doctor's lounge? Let me tell you, those kids ain't eatin' oat bran, honey. They're loading up on steak, shrimp the size of your fist, ice cream, pie, and home-made biscuits.

Don't get me wrong, I'm thankful for doctors, nurses, surgeons, and all those folks. Lord knows I've spent so much time in the local hospital they run when they see me coming, I'm so accident-prone and so well-insured. However, I can't help but recall the hilarious scene from one of my favorite movies, Woody Allen's *Sleeper.* A man from the 1970s, who has been frozen for several hundred years, is thawed. His doctors present him with a gigantic hot fudge sundae. He turns it down and asks for a bowl of wheat germ or fruit instead. His doctors chuckle, "Oh, we now know that fats and hot fudge are the most important nutrients in life. Fruits and vegetables are the cause of cancer," or something like that, and Mr. Sleeper picks up a spoon and indulges himself until he turns green. *I wish.*

Really, do any of us follow the advice of our doctors? I certainly don't, and I'm proud to say this defiance runs in my family. When I was nine, my father took me to see an allergist *(most likely my mother had a severed spine and couldn't drive, because that's the only reason any father in the late Sixties would have ushered his child out of the house without maternal supervision).* My dad, whom I love dearly, is not a patient man. He marched me into the allergist's office. The doctor did his thing, which took about a minute and a half, and told my father I still had allergies and asthma. He then questioned my father, who is an extremely bright man, as to the intelligence of both parents smoking three packs a day in a house where a child has severe asthma. My father didn't say a word, he just nodded and smiled tersely. Let me tell you, we never went back to that allergist, and my parents continued to smoke at home. We soon moved to a temperate zone where the lack of seasonal pollen improved my condition immensely. *Doctors, shmoctors,* I'm sure my dad thought, *I'll fix this myself!*

With that shining example of parental guidance, I soon learned **Big Girl Secret Tip #11:** *Doctors fully expect you to reinterpret their advice and tailor it to your personal situation. If your doctor had intended for you to actually lose weight, he would have written you a prescription for an all-expense paid, two-week* *stay at a luxurious spa. Let's face it, if your physician has seen no visible effort on your part to lose weight over the past fifteen years, is your size truly a concern or is he merely fulfilling his Doctor Vow and his financial commitment to his organic vegetable farm investment partners?*

A Case in Point: While most reasonably intelligent adults choose to live in a climate that is conducive to their particular health needs, against the advice of my personal cadre of physicians, I unwisely make my home in the Buckle of the Pollen and Allergy Belt. Consequently my Ear, Nose and Throat guy has kindly named the new wing of his office in my honor. To say I've had a few sinus surgeries is to say that Babe Ruth hit a couple home runs. Anyhow, I have *IRREFUTABLE PROOF* that my Big Girl existence contributed to saving my life. Several years ago, my sinus doctor decided that he would like to unzip my head at my scalp, peel it back and drill out my ethmoid sinus, where an entire colony of nasty bacteria resided in a state of gangrenous bliss.

I'm in his office, discussing the procedure and the fact that I'll be the hands-down winner of the Frankenstein Look Alike Contest at Halloween, when my doctor rubs his face and frowns. "What we'll have to figure out," he says, "is where to find the fat that we'll pack into your drilled-out sinus, so your head won't have a big dent in it." I blinked and was silent, which for me is exceedingly rare. I'm no surgeon, mind you, but I'm thinking, *Ok, here's a Big Girl with Extra Padding, being told by her physician that he needs to find some FAT to pack into her head. Is this the man I should entrust to use power tools near my brain?*

Of course the doctor was only musing out loud. He did indeed find a rather nice pocket of fat on my abdomen and transported it to its new home in the center of my forehead.

Maybe I'm psychic and knew this day would come, thus being a Big Girl definitely saved me from joining the circus as Bunkie the Dented Forehead Wonder.

Which brings me to **Big Girl Secret Tip #12:** *You never know when being a Big Girl will save your life, so rip up those Body Mass Index charts and pass the chocolate cake!*

This next section is quite technical, so please put down that candy bar and pay close attention. *(Did I just say that? I'm so sorry!)* We will now discuss, in depth, the Art of Weighing In at the Doctor's Office, or as some of our Southern Big Girl friends say, Hangin' the Ham on the Hook. Medical scales are the Vile Enemy and are to be avoided at all costs. When you go to the State Fair with a Cute Boy, or for you more mature Big Girls, a Man of Advanced Age and Unimaginable Wealth *(see Chapter Eight, Relationships)*, you can always steer clear of the Guess Your Weight Game by suggesting that you ride the go-carts. Regrettably, there are no go-cart distractions at the doctor's office.

When it is absolutely unavoidable to weigh yourself, like when the nurse gets you in a headlock and insists you're gonna step on that scale or she'll come at you with a number twelve scalpel, you must focus and propel yourself into Big Girl Auto-Pilot Mode. You must mentally prepare to deal with the Vile Enemy, which means you must first undergo basic training. Get into those closets, now, ladies, and identify your lightest articles of clothing … sleeveless tops and spandex shorts are usually perfect options, and sandals are the preferred footwear of choice. Oh, good grief, I don't care if it's snowing, wear a coat for God's sake and get over it!

Approach the Vile Enemy with caution and *PUT DOWN THAT PURSE AND TAKE OFF THOSE SANDALS! ARE YOU AN IDIOT, PRIVATE?* **Big Girl Secret Tip #13:** *NEVER*

WEIGH YOURSELF WEARING SHOES OR HOLDING YOUR HANDBAG!

Avoid all accessories, including headbands, jewelry, watches, eyeglasses, contact lenses, dental implants, and artificial limbs *(don't worry, the nurse will assist you)*. In certain cases it may be advisable to *go commando* to trick the Vile Enemy into believing that you maintained the same exact weight as last year. Trust me on this. You can go without underwear for a few hours ... we're talking survival tactics here, missy. Keep your eyes on the *PRIZE!*

The most difficult facet of Weighing In is that indefinite, uncomfortable time you must wait while the Vile Enemy toys with you, while it flirts with which evil number it shall choose. At this moment you should recite to yourself a preselected mantra, such as *"Dairy Queen is right around the corner"* or *"Make that a Triple Extra Value Size and hurry!"* When the Vile Enemy finally chooses its lottery winner and the nurse notes your number, now is not the time to be faint. You must stand steadfast. You cannot waver. You cannot cringe or avert your eyes. Look 'er dead in the eye, and say, *"Cut the three-fourths of a pound crap. Go ahead and make it a full pound higher. You know you want to."*

Which brings us to **Big Girl Secret Tip #14:** *It is advisable to form a professional relationship with a qualified orthopedic surgeon. Suck it up and face the music, Big Girl. Your knees are gonna give out from all that Extra Padding, and when they do, you're gonna need good drugs. Find a Cute Doctor because it makes those cortisone shots a helluva lot more bearable. Trust me on this.*

Although no one, by any stretch of the imagination, would consider me an athlete, I am pretty physically active. Buying all this food and lugging it into the house each week is no small task, friends. I have a young child and consequently chase him around most of the day. I have two sets of stairs in my house *(my husband's idea of forced exercise),* and I often find myself volunteering for activities where I'm required to stand on my feet a lot, which means my ankles often resemble bowling balls and my fingers look like Little Smokies®. When it comes to the pain in my load-bearing joints, I have two choices: I could lose weight, which according to my orthopedist would reduce the *stress on those puppies at a 4:1 ratio (but the process would cause me to become an axe murderer);* or I can maintain my current weight and take non-steroidal anti-inflammatory drugs (NSAIDs) as the good Lord intended, with an occasional pain pill thrown in for good measure.

Being the Intelligent Big Girl that I am, I realize my limitations. If I succumbed to a weight loss program, I'm starin' down 15-25 in the slammer for chopping up everyone around me who is eating foods on my forbidden list. A much wiser choice is to keep those NSAIDs refilled and memorize my orthopedist's phone number. Don't you agree? Of course you do!

Sometimes physicians are stubborn when it comes to the prescribing of medication, and this is particularly true for Big Girls. That is why I'm here to share with you the latest findings from the **Big Girl School of Pharmacology:**

1) If two ibuprofen are the prescribed dose, then six or eight are much more likely to dissolve your Big Girl Pain in half the time, as in *right now, dammit.*

2) Narcotics prescribed for dental surgery and other relatively minor medical mishaps should *never* be tossed away. Neither should they be loaned out. Trust me, you will need

them *(see Chapter Three, Exercise & Its Avoidance)*.

3) Two Top-Shelf margaritas and a handful of NSAIDs are exactly what the Big Girl Pharmacological Expert ordered to dispose of headaches, asshole bosses, and the knowledge that your parents are coming for a three-week stay.

4) For those occasional sleepless nights, a triple dose of cough syrup added to a half bottle of wine will fix you right up. **Big Girl Secret Tip #15:** *Before administering this therapy, it is advisable to leave your boss a voice mail message and inform him that you believe you have contracted West Nile virus and you need to stay home.*

5) Anti-depressants are all good and fine if you enjoy the physical impossibility of achieving orgasm. I've never seen a case of the blues that couldn't be cured by a house call from the Keebler Elves®.

As our intense pharmacological research has shown, Big Girls only require a physician for major surgery or prescription refills, unless they're married to a pharmacist, which I highly recommend. Why waste time in a doctor's office, when I have at my disposal my Big Girl Friend Who Is a Hypochondriacal Medical Expert? This girl has every medical Web site known to man bookmarked on her computer. She can quote you chapter and verse about illnesses and their symptoms, as well as their remedies. With one brief look, she can determine whether that strange red spot on your arm is a melanoma *(oh my gosh, hack that thing off right now)*, or just a mark where your sister clawed you because you ate the last chocolate chip cookie in the house— *again*.

I rarely bother calling the doctor. I just shout at my Big Girl Friend Who is a Hypochondriacal Medical Expert, because chances are she's shared my identical symptoms and received a miraculous healing. I swear this girl cured herself of tuberculosis, heart trouble, and Parkinson's disease, all in the same week. The insurance companies better watch out, because we Big Girls are organized. Forget your PPOs and HMOs ... we're starting a PBBMEO: a Preferred Big Butt Medical Expert Organization. You simply dial a toll-free number, enter your password, and we'll bring you a six-pack of Little Debbies or a handful of pain pills, depending upon your specific malady, of course.

What I don't understand is that in all my years of seeing doctors, and I've seen some doozies, let me tell you, only my orthopedist has ever faced me about my weight. He pretty much got up *in* my face and said I'd be pulling myself around in a little cart if I didn't do something drastic. He scared me so much I abstained from ice cream for 48 hours. Sure, a few of my previous physicians commented, "Well, you surely know proper nutrition and the benefits of weight loss. You're a smart girl." *Hello.* This may surprise you ... *it's not working.*

As a doctor, if I spent all that time in med school and worked a 400-hour week with only Wednesdays off for golf, my idea of a peaceful day at the office would not include lecturing a Big Girl about her size, especially if I wished to leave with my head intact. But seriously, how many Big Girls out there see physicians who tell it like it is? All you doctor-types, put down your free pharmaceutical ink pens, stop writing me that hate mail this instant. What I mean is, why don't you give us the Real Low-Down about our weight? Instead of the anatomical illustrations that decorate your office, why not hang up a couple of photos depicting hip-replacement surgery or the inside of a stroke victim's clotted artery, or play a video in your waiting room of someone sustaining a heart attack after climbing three flights of stairs with a bucket of chicken and a six-pack? This is not an attempt to lay the blame on someone else. I'm really good at that and, believe me, you'll know when it happens. But I'm so engrossed in what I perceive to be my comfortable, overweight lifestyle, so insulated by my size and by my denial, maybe I need a big-ass medical shock to snap me into reality. And who better to shock me than the folks who have routinely seen the medical equivalent of the Apocalypse and cleaned up the mess? *Go figure.*

Well, I've certainly read the medical profession the riot act, haven't I? Let me step off my extra-large soapbox and apologize to everyone in the healthcare community; everyone who ever entertained, if only for a millisecond, the desire to help others through medicine; everyone who wishes to become a health-care professional in the future; and all the little kids who play doctor at home ... I may need you if this Big Girl bursitis kicks back in.

It's time now to take a spin on the most entertaining medical whirly-gig that is my life, otherwise known as At War with the World as Your Hormones Race Out of Control. *Let's review* **Big Girl Secret Tip #16:** *Marry by age 30, have 2.3 kids by age 35, then after the birth of your second child, as the OB-GYN is tidying things up down there, grab him by the neck and calmly but firmly demand the immediate removal of all your internal female organs. If your doctor refuses, hell, you're under anesthesia, grab a hose and suck those puppies out! DO IT! Trust me, you do not want to experience peri-menopause, menopause, or any part of anything with the word "pause" in it. Why do you think they call it men-o-pause? Because you sure as hell don't want to have anything to do with a man and his idea of a good time* *when your internal body temperature is 212 degrees and you've just crawled into the freezer for relief!*

As a Big Girl, I carry around a tad more estrogen in my body than my fit girlfriend counterparts. On my 35th birthday, I woke up to the shrieking alarm that was my body clock and realized it was time to have a baby. Thank God I had the foresight to have already reeled in a husband, or this decision might have posed a problem. But in any case, I promptly visited my OB-GYN and informed her of my intent. She first picked herself off the floor after my announcement that I could simply make my body and my husband's sperm do what I wanted, at will. Then she informed me that I might experience difficulties of many untold natures, most of them due to an excess of estrogen in my body, because I was a *Big Girl.*

When I did get pregnant, I can safely attest that it was beyond a doubt the only time in my life that I ate healthy and was motivated not to overeat. *What an amazing concept.* You should try it, really! I am convinced that this determination to take care of my unborn child used all my physical and mental power, rendering me incapable of withstanding the evil forces of the solar system. Thus, I subsequently endured every possible side effect of pregnancy that anyone in the History of the Universe has ever suffered, multiplied by a factor of ten. I irritated my physicians to no end.

I know this for a fact, because while I was still in the hospital after my C-section, they informed me that due to my Big Girl blood pressure issues, I was no longer a candidate for birth control pills. They took great pains to describe to me, in precise medical terminology, several newly discovered, mysterious pregnancy side effects that a person with my extra-large frame and whiny constitution would no doubt experience. They told me in no uncertain terms that if I became pregnant again, I'd be forced to come in five times a week for blood pressure monitoring and pelvic exams. *We're a happy, one-child household, friends.*

Pregnancy for Big Girls is a unique adventure. Try writing a check at the grocery store when you can't step up to the counter because your belly is bigger than even you, a Big Girl, could imagine. Your hand is numb from carpal tunnel syndrome, your palms itch, and your eyes can't focus, because this growing child inside you is sucking every ounce of nutrition from your body. *Oh, but wait, there's more!* There are no Big Girl maternity clothes, so you lurk in front of the discount store, waiting to break into the Just My Size delivery truck and snatch those rare 5X shirts and shorts before anyone else can grab 'em.

Because you're a Big Girl, your medical team will inform you that you'll develop gestational diabetes. But when you don't, they won't believe it, and they stare at you like you're from Planet P. When your blood pressure goes up *(and it will, when that danged doctor examines you in the eighth month and tries to turn that sucker around so you can avoid a C-section)*, get ready. You will most likely be on blood pressure medicine for the rest of your natural born days, unless you succumb to a Weight Loss Program That Works, and to date, I've found no such animal.

My doctors insisted I visit their office every week and be strapped into something that resembled an electric chair, to monitor my blood pressure and the baby's heartbeat. *Gee, what fun. Thanks. I had absolutely nothing better to do than sit here with my good friends Mister and Missus Electrode for an hour.* And there's no getting up to pee when you're in that chair, and **let's review** how much a pregnant woman pees … I had to go so badly one time on the way to a specialist's office, I pulled

over at a Krystal in the middle of the projects. My own husband refused to get out of the car with me but nobody would
have dared to take on a Big Pregnant Girl with Whoop-Ass
Attitude. No, ma'am, I wasn't at all concerned.

After my son was delivered safely and proved to be the
Heaven on Earth that everyone tells you about, reality sinks in.
The Post Natal Depression Period arrives, and I'm not talking
modern art, here. You become a walking bag of hormones and
cry for no apparent reason at diaper commercials. Your
abdomen feels like an acupuncturist's pincushion from the C-
section staples and strange, resultant twinges. Only the baby is
sleeping, and when your husband complains, *"I'm so tired my
stomach hurts,"* you want to shove him into the oven and eat
him for dinner, except you aren't allowed to lift anything heav-
ier than your infant.

This goes on for about five years, except for the lifting part,
and then, *joy unspeakable,* you enter peri-menopause, which
can last, say, for roughly ten years, followed by menopause,
that can drag out for about another three to five, according to
various and sundry medical experts who enjoy playing sick calendar jokes on female patients. To further clarify:
peri-menopause means "before the change," and it apparently
is much worse than the real deal, if you listen to the talk show
experts. Lord knows, I do. Peri-menopause is when lots of the
hormonal "stuff" happens. If you can survive it without going
to jail, and actually enter menopause, it's all downhill from
there. There is a vast amount of research *(ok, only a folder or
two, but do you really care?)* indicating that Big Girls endure ten
times more suffering in peri-menopause than do our tragically
fit girl colleagues. Why? It's that ol' surplus of estrogen thing
again, because **let's review:** fat contains estrogen. *Now do you
get it?*

This brings us to the critical **Big Girl Secret Tip #17:** *Prior to entering peri-menopause, if you ignored our expert advice in Secret Tip #16, you'd best buy yourself a new 400-ton industrial strength air conditioner, seven thousand pounds of chocolate, and a few cases of red wine. Your body will heat up to its maximum geothermal limit and you risk spontaneous combustion. You're gonna be cranky and you're gonna scream at all humanoids, random governmental institutions, and the dog for no apparent reason. You think you were sleep-deprived with a newborn, just wait. You'll sweat so much at night, you're gonna need your child's waterproof sheets. Your life is gonna be one long, never-ending, menstrual period and you'll need Extra Super Duper Wide Plus tampons and Panty Liners with Big-Ass Concorde Wings by the truckload. For TEN to THIRTEEN years.*

Do we have your attention, now? *Yes, I thought so.* This is the only time in your Big Girl life when your breasts, that Big Girl Asset whose proportion and beauty skinny lasses can only dream about, become evil. We're not talking run-of-the-mill PMS tenderness, girls. We're talking you gotta dust the furniture *á la* Diana, Roman Goddess of the Hunt, with your mammaries fully exposed, to avoid the peri-menopausal side effect that takes place when even your most lightweight clothing *(see Weigh-In, previously)* causes debilitating pain if it touches your size 48DD instruments of desire and human survival.

Peri-menopausal Big Girls have been known to bite the heads off live chickens when enraged by something so trivial as a microscopic piece of lint on the floor of the recently vacuumed den. I personally attended an intervention for a Hormonal Big Girl Friend of mine, when she baked her family the world's most beautiful carrot cake, then attacked her spouse with the electric mixer after he tried to lick the beaters that she had previously claimed as her own. Another Big Girl Friend of mine suffered such severe hot flashes, she set the air conditioner to 22 degrees Fahrenheit. Her husband subsequently suffered frostbite on three toes. Because she was in peri-menopause and overheard him complain about the pain in his digits, she volunteered to remove them, free of charge, with the paring knife.

Unless you possess the resources to pack yourself off to a private island for about ten years, you've got to figure out how to survive the Menopausal Decades. My Big Girl Friend Who Takes Swift Medical Action has signed up at a local hospital to be the first patient in town to have her endometrial lining singed off with the medical equivalent of a curling iron. When I informed my husband that I expected to approach the peak of my peri-menopausal state at the exact same time our son would hit puberty, he did something shocking and unheard of in the annals of men: he called my OB-GYN. He made me an appointment, and instructed that doctor to "fix" things.

There is nothing I enjoy less than a visit to the friendly neighborhood OB-GYN. As if it's not insulting enough that Big Girls can't fit into the expensive, plush robes found in expensive, plush hotel rooms, we sure as hell can't fit into the gowns at the OB-GYN's office. Even the beauty salon has Big Girl haircut capes to fit around Big Girl necks, but not the OB-GYN, no ma'am. It's not like they *don't know* ... I've been there for mammograms every year for the last ten years, so it's not like they've never seen me with my shirt off, good grief!

Now my OB-GYN is very competent and a saint, considering everything I've put her through. She can see through me like the clear wrap on a Twinkie. I described my peri-menopausal symptoms to her in great detail, hoping for at the very least a modicum of reaction on her part. But all she did was nod *yes* and purse her lips. When I informed her of my conviction that there were probably fibroid tumors in my uterus the size of Kansas City, she smiled and reminded me that she'd seen nothing out of the ordinary during my very recent annual exam, an annual exam complete with ultrasounds, where ultrasounds really should never dare to go. Then she patted me on the arm and said, "Look, for a woman your age ... all of this is normal. If it gets so bad that you're having a period less than every 21 days, we can do something about it. But as you know, you're a *Big Girl,* and some of the typical options we might have are not open to us right now. Take care!" Less than every 21 days? Lordy be, *I really don't think so!* WHERE IS MY CHOCOLATE?

Chapter Eight

Relationships & Money

Some of you Big Girls might feel compelled at this point to comment, *"Hmmm, this seems like quite a trivial little chapter, since every Big Girl knows that without Money, there can be no Relationship."* Well, you're exactly right, of course, but hang with me for a sec, please. When you become a Famous Author and write your own book, you can discuss anything you like, ok?

Big Girls face seemingly insurmountable odds when it comes to sustaining Relationships. It's not that we don't want them. With the exception of my friend, the Big Bad-Ass Girl Who is Doing Time and prefers everyone to keep their hands to themselves, this is rarely the case. No, the sad truth of the matter is that most Big Girls dream of Relationships, long-lasting love, a Knight in Shining Armor who drives an expensive sports car, or at least very good sex. But this is hard to come by in a world where body ideals are based on a genetic mutation between a pretzel stick and a female humanoid with silicone breast implants.

We lifelong Big Girls learn early on that we are different *(TRANSLATION: UNDESIRABLE)* and that no self-respecting people on earth, except our mothers and our doctors, would dare give us a second look. This uniform rejection typically begins in elementary school, at recess. It is precisely at this point in our lives that our Big Girl skin begins to thicken, because virtually everyone believes that Big Girls carry *Super Ultra Death-Ray Cooties That You Can't Survive,* and neither boy nor girl wants any part of *that.* I used to take Nancy Drew to recess with me, and we'd hide behind a large oak tree on the playground. This method worked well until I had read all the Nancy Drew books at least three times over. Thank God for the Trixie Belden series, or I never would have survived.

In middle school *(what we used to call junior high, so much more exciting),* the raging hormones of puberty set in and Things Begin to Change. You still have boys and girls running around on the playground, but this time it's akin to a Shakespearean screwball comedy, where you can't possibly keep up with who just broke up with whom, who likes so-and-so but can't bring herself to tell him, and which boy has taken up residence behind my oak tree to practice French-kissing with willing participants who are looked on as "fast."

As a Big Girl, my role in this charade was a tad strange, but welcome, in any case. I was now viewed as something other than just a *Super Ultra Death-Ray Cootie* carrier. I became the Big Girl Love Advisor to my classmates. Now this in itself is hysterically ironic, in that as a *Big Girl* I had not the slightest experience with boys or love or kissing or going with anyone, except that I once had a boyfriend for three days in second grade, until we moved away. It took me five trips to the candy store to get over him, let me tell you. In any case, there I was, standing around hoping to get my tree back and read about

Trixie's latest case, when adolescents of both sexes began to confide in me, seeking my counsel in their respective romantic conquests.

Now that I'm of advanced age and extreme wisdom, I look back and realize that every middle school student since the Dawn of Time looks and acts like a Consummate Geek. I have my yearbook to prove it. Even the popular kids, thanks to braces, growth spurts, and budding body parts that don't quite seem to fit anywhere, were anything but poised. But at the time, there were obvious No-Geek boundaries and Major Geek Denial, so for me to become the Big Girl Love Advisor to the entire seventh grade, we're talkin' *I HAVE ARRIVED*, baby. *I AM HOT!*

Despite my intense desire to fit into the middle school social strata, something deep inside my Big Girl soul realized how dim-witted these people were to come to me for advice. It was precisely at this point that I developed the ultimate Big Girl tools for Lifetime Survival, Sarcasm, and Revenge.

Which brings me to **Big Girl Secret Tip #18:** *It is absolutely essential for Big Girls to learn the art of sarcasm and revenge and their proper usage. I don't care if you have to watch every Rodney Dangerfield and Don Rickles movie ever made or take a class at a community college to learn these higher arts. You cannot survive a single day as a Big Girl without the use of sarcasm and revenge.*

Let's review one of my personal experiences: Kristen, the most blonde and beautiful girl in the entire middle school *(of course she's a cheerleader and we absolutely hate her, but right now she's coming to us for advice, so hold that thought)* is going with Dusty. *Why* she is going with Dusty, who from his appearance has not recently bathed with soap and whose idea of a cool fashion accessory is a puka shell necklace, is a mystery to me,

but it's her love life. Anyhow, Kristen just overheard a playground conversation between Janet and Beth Ann, and has
learned that the most popular boy in school, Ronnie, is having
a boy-girl party at his house on Friday night. Kristen is concerned. She has not yet been invited and it is Thursday, so the
prospects aren't looking good.

Kristen approaches the Big Girl Love Advisor, who is
presently counting ladybugs on the dirt next to the fence, and
poses her question: Should she dump Dusty and his puka
shells, right here, right now, and declare undying love to
Ronnie in order to snag a party invite, or should she tell the
school nurse she's sick so she can phone her mother and ask if
she can have her own boy-girl party, and invite everyone who
is planning to attend Ronnie's soirée?

This is a tough case for the Big Girl Love Advisor, her rep-
utation is on the line. She eyes Kristen up and down and notes
that Kristen is perspiring a great deal more than a popular girl
should. In fact, Kristen almost stinks, she's perspiring so much,
and she has a pimple on her nose the size of Minneapolis. Big
Girl Love Advisor glances up and notes that a line has formed
behind Kristen, prospective clients who are much less odifer-
ous and pimple-laden, patiently waiting their turn. Big Girl
Love Advisor knows for a fact that Kristen's new *inamorata*,
Ronnie, is at this very moment behind the oak tree, French-
kissing Kristen's best friend, Donna Sue. Kristen and Donna
Sue are charter members of the Bitchy Middle School
Cheerleader Society. Big Girl suddenly flashes back to the
beginning of the school year, when Kristen remarked that Big
Girl was so fat she couldn't even *pay* a boy to kiss her behind
the oak tree. Big Girl Love Advisor takes a deep breath and
decides to have a little fun.

"Kristen, the nurse can see you're not sick. And who'll

know if you're really having a party or not? I mean, your parents are divorced. I heard your mom lets you do whatever you want. Go break up with Dusty and tell everybody you're having a boy-girl party tomorrow night at seven, because I heard that Ronnie's party starts at seven-thirty. Then get Donna Sue to tell Ronnie that you broke up with Dusty because you like him better. Hurry!"

The smile on Kristen's face could not be any wider. Gratitude to the Big Girl Love Advisor spills out of her mouth like water over Niagara Falls. Big Girl Love Advisor nods silently and informs her next client, *"Hang on a sec, something good is about to go down."*

All eyes follow Kristen as she marches over to Dusty. After a few angst-ridden words, along the order of *"I don't like you anymore, we're breaking up,"* Kristen marches away in triumph and Dusty kicks the ground. Kristen moves to the basketball court and announces that a boy-girl party will be held at her home at seven the following evening; that her mother's boyfriend will be in town, thus all adults will be otherwise engaged; and that she's taking requests for her guests' favorite party foods. *"And,"* Kristen says coyly, *"we have a Coke machine at our house, like the one at the drugstore, so we can play Spin-the-Bottle!"*

The buzz on the playground is deafening at the prospect of a boy-girl party featuring Spin-the-Bottle with minimal adult supervision. Kristen skips the steps of enhanced popularity over to a group of girls and inquires as to the whereabouts of Donna Sue. Big Girl Love Advisor goes in for the kill. She calls out to Kristen that she remembers seeing Donna Sue near the oak tree. Kristen is momentarily surprised to learn that her best friend would go anywhere near the Seventh Grade French-Kissing Station, but walks closer to investigate. A terrible scream pierces the air; Kristen has just witnessed Ronnie, the New Boy of her Dreams, with his hand down Donna Sue's shirt and his tongue in Donna Sue's mouth. Kristen stomps away in tears. As she approaches the jungle gym, she spies Dusty, her ex, with his arm around Roxanne, the new girl from Florida, who, according to all the boys, is not only "fast," she "races." Big Girl Love Advisor closes shop for the day, satisfied that even though she can't pay a boy to kiss her, Kristen's charmed life is now miserable, at least for a few hours.

My role as Big Girl Love Advisor continued throughout high school, until my senior year. I counseled countless, tortured friends on the most intimate details of their love lives, like I gave a rat's ass, but it afforded me a measure of Control, Power, and Respect that I otherwise might not have enjoyed. I excelled at Meaningful Looks of Sorrow, Deep Moments of Great Anguish, and Ecstatic Jubilatory Smiles as my friends relayed their escapades on the highway of high school love. Meanwhile, I selected various Cute Boys from afar, boys on whom I maintained crushes of gigantic proportions, but I never shared my Crush List with anyone. God forbid my friends find out and make me the laughingstock of the entire school.

At some point, a crush on one of my list-people turned into a close friendship, which then led to dating. This brings me to **Big Girl Secret Tip #19:** *If, after the second or third date with a Cute Boy, he hasn't attempted to French-kiss you or feel you up, he's most likely gay, so don't waste any more time. Trust me on this, I speak from experience.*

I spent nearly two years of my life dating a closet gay. Although he was a barrel of laughs and I enjoyed, for the first time ever, real dates to the movies and to parties, and even to the Prom, it was frustrating. If you think you're a Confused Big Girl when nobody takes an interest in you, it's even worse when you date someone for the better part of two years and you spend a lot of time convincing yourself that he is *so nice,* he respects you *so much,* that's why he would never take any liberties.

In our desperation to be loved, Big Girls turn off their Gaydar and often miss subtle clues as to the sexual orientation of our boyfriends. I know I certainly did. His favorite music consisted of Barry Manilow, Bette Midler, and, *shock,* Queen. I just thought they were really good musicians and that my boyfriend had eclectic tastes. Many of our friends were in the artsy-fartsy crowd, so it was perfectly acceptable to quote famous alternative-lifestyle authors and dress in drag on occasion, or talk non-stop about Broadway plays. We attended different colleges but saw each other during breaks. After a while, I began to wonder. Is he revolted by the sight of me and too chicken to split? Or even worse ... *does he have another girlfriend?*

One day a good friend of mine casually suggested, by screaming in a very shrill voice, that I might be wasting my time, and that I might be taking part in a Cover-Up of Gigantic Gay Proportions. Though I knew my boyfriend sincerely cared about me, in his own Sick User way, it was time to call it quits and face the prospect of Big Girl Loneliness once more. I dropped him a *Dear John* letter, because I was fed up with the whole situation, and I figured if he didn't have the guts to confess his obvious sexual preferences to his own girlfriend, then I didn't owe him the time of day. Deep down I had always thought it would be fun to write somebody a *Dear John* letter, and seeing as how this might be my only chance to play that particular game, I knocked that letter off in about three minutes flat. We've never spoken since, but I hope he's had a nice life, whatever his persuasion.

Having a relationship under my belt *(oops, forgot. Big Girls don't wear belts, please substitute "big shirt")* ultimately gave me the confidence to seek more relationships. After all, I was now no longer a Boyfriend Virgin *(let's don't get too technical here, ok?).* I was broken in, by all credible social standards, which meant that someone, at some time in my life, wanted me by his side. *It could happen again,* I realized. *Stranger things have taken place.* I prepared for Mister Right, with new makeup, a different wardrobe, a promising career in the exciting world of public utilities, but no new eating habits. Therein lies the rub, I guess. Over the course of the next four or five years, I dated. I swear I did. At least twice! There was a pretty serious relationship with a high school friend that turned a little scary when he informed me that I was good marriage material, he had a great job, and his dream was to have at least six children. Can you say, *"Run as fast as your flabby Big Girl legs will go?"* Sure, I knew you could.

This brings me to **Big Girl Secret Tip #20:** *The only acceptable method to deal with Misery of Any Kind is to run away, fast. You'd be pretty danged amazed at the Top Land Speed of a Motivated Big Girl. Don't like your present relationship? Having difficulty in your job? Need a change of scenery? Why not make it permanent? Pack those bags, fill up the gas tank, and head out. Just leave those troubles behind, literally, and start over in an exciting, new venue where you are certain to become the Life of the Party and Make it Big (not like Big Girl big, but Successful). Make sure to properly name your pain, the reason why you are leaving ... it is <u>never</u> your fault.*

I've started over so many times in my life, you'd swear I was in the Witness Protection Program. Wiping the slate clean means you must first regress and make new friends, and become the Big Girl Love Advisor again for a little while, until these new friends realize you are a Very Funny Big Girl with a Pretty Face Who is Lonely. At this critical point, your buds will introduce you to all sorts of eligible scum, like the previously mentioned Mister Quadruple Lack of Personality from Hell, and Mister Bad Toupee. What you really need is to hook up with a pharmacist who can dispense free anti-depressants, so you can make it through the umpteenth boring job in your string of career successes, but that doesn't always materialize.

Here is **Big Girl Secret Tip #21**, straight out: *Skip the dating services, skip the blind dates arranged by your thin friends with a sick sense of humor. Skip the Personals. You have two choices: **a**) put on some fishnet stockings and hot pants (ignore Ultimate Fashion No-No #2, temporarily) and carry a "WILL DATE FOR FOOD" sign, or **b**) go to church.*

Yes, Big Girls of the World, I am here to proclaim that church is the best-kept dating secret in the Western World. "Why?" you may ask. One does not necessarily associate the word "church" with finding one's true love across the veritable smoke-filled room amid alcoholic beverages, unless of course, you are Catholic. Then all bets are off, because those guys can swing some serious incense and put away the wine. I'm quite serious here. Church is the only way to go on the Highway to True Love.

Here is Why Big Girls Should Go to Church to Find the Perfect Husband:

1) *Heinous criminals and serial killers do not routinely attend church.*

2) *The Boss won't make a pass at you.* The minister is most likely married, or celibate.

3) *The once-a-week thing keeps wardrobe expenditures to a*

minimum. So what if you wore that cute outfit two weeks ago. That was *two weeks ago.* You think anybody noticed? Accessorize and move on.

4) *Catcalls, insults, and fat jokes are not allowed in church.* Unless you belong to the Church Ladies Society. You're not their type until you're married and famous for your tuna casserole with the crushed potato chips on top.

5) *Your eligible single-man radar works exceptionally well* in a setting where the attendees are young families with sticky, screaming children and old people who insist that walkers are the definitive fashion accessory.

6) *Choir robes are the great body-type equalizer.* If you join the choir, you can stop worrying altogether about your wardrobe and your weight. Believe me, nobody in any choir ever looked slim in a green robe, ok? Plus, from the choir loft, you can look down on all the Eligible Single Men and determine which ones may soon evolve into Mister Bad Toupee or which ones have hairy necks. *This is critical.*

7) *Free dating and dinner service.* Your church-mates will take pity on you and fix you up with the Eligible Single Men, by inviting you both for dinner in their homes. This is a pretty good gig if you can get it, because other than making nice with the sticky, screaming children, there are no embarrassing first-date restaurant conversation pauses. Things can get really lively when the sticky, screaming children throw their food on the wall, *what a hoot that is,* especially if the Eligible Single Man competes with the children, you get a Neanderthal Behavior Alert, as well as

a free meal. And Eligible Single Men can, in this low-key, "Try Before you Buy" setting, determine whether or not they wish to take you to a restaurant on their nickel, or drive you to a motel and remove all your clothes, then go out for dessert. Either way, you win.

8) *Booking the chapel.* By attending church, when you meet Mister Right, and *trust me, you will,* you have an "in" with the Padre for first dibs on the calendar to schedule your wedding ceremony. *Eyes on the Prize, ladies. Eyes on the Prize!*

After nearly three decades of Big Girl Desperation, I had all but given up. But the Angel of the Lord sent down my husband, smack in the middle of a church pew ... a perfect, wonderful man who loves me for who I am ... and now look at us. I'm a Married Big Girl and he's the King of the Hen-Pecked Husbands. But isn't that what True Love is all about? Yes, it is, and don't you forget it or there'll be hell to pay! Seriously, all Big Girls find True Love before they die. Doesn't that make you feel better?

We haven't yet addressed some of the more awkward moments of Big Girl Relationships, such as the *Rules of the Game.* I suggest you clip out this section, make about a thousand copies, and distribute it to every man you know. Wait, am I an *idiot?* You'd think I was doing this out of the goodness of my heart and don't need the money! Tell them to buy their own copies!

Here are the **Absolute Rules of The Game When Making Romantic Advances with a Big Girl:**

1) Big Girls' brassieres have tungsten steel reinforcements and

possess not two, but *THREE* sets of hooks. This can be a little tricky, but hey, guys, steal a bra from your granny and practice in the comfort of your own home before dating a Big Girl. And steer clear when that baby pops open, ok, or you might hurt yourself from the backlash.

2) It is never acceptable to fondly pinch or nickname any Lipid Enhancement *(TRANSLATION: ROLL OF FAT)* on any part of a Big Girl's body, period.

3) Proper lighting is imperative. Big Girls, unless they are real sickos, favor complete and total darkness. I mean, it's ok to light a candle to set the mood, but when a Big Girl is expected to engage in various states of undress, those damned lights better be *OFF!*

4) Chocolate and red wine, two essential Big Girl Food Groups, make the difference between a Night You'll Never Forget and It Ain't Gonna Happen in This Lifetime, Buster.

5) When you host a Big Girl at your Personal Love Shack, remember that if a Big Girl doesn't snack every two hours, she will keel over and die. For once in your life, go to the grocery store and fill up your cart with something besides beer and pretzels. *FYI,* celery is not a snack. And if you go downstairs to make yourself a sandwich, don't come back up unless you've got an extra one for me and it's made with real mayo, ok?

Now that we've enlightened Big Girls on how to find Mister Right, let's proceed to a hush-hush topic: Breaking Up. Do you think that after waiting decades to finally identify, bait, and catch Mister Right, a Big Girl worth her weight in potato chips would do something as asinine as dump him?

Here are the Only Acceptable Situations When a Big Girl Should Dump a Man:

1) If he practices an Alternative Lifestyle that you really just can't stomach (an aversion to women or living with his mother both qualify)

2) If he is broke

3) If he is serving Life and there is no way to get your hands on his estate

There is absolutely no other reason in the world, Big Girl, to unhitch your wagon from the Caravan of Romantic Happiness. I don't want to hear it. And now that we've clarified that subject, let's talk Money. Big Girls need truckloads of it to be truly happy. Why? Have you ever walked through a Big Girl Designer Clothing store? Anything with the phrase "Plus-sized" or "Generous cut" means you might as well go to the bank, withdraw all your cash, and plop it on the counter if you want to wear that outfit, honey. Big Girls are extremely high maintenance. Hair removal products, cell phones with unlimited minutes, anti-depressants, and the best chocolates are not cheap, jacko.

Let's review the **Big Girl Secret Test to Determine an Eligible Man's Wealth and Marriageability:**

1) Dinners at expensive restaurants are an excellent sign. If he

insists you go dutch after the second date, he's cheap and you will be miserable for all eternity. Drop him like a hot potato.

2) European sports cars, particularly the convertible variety, are way, way up there. SUVs are acceptable, if they are brand-spanking new and have DVD players, so you can lounge in the backseat on long trips and watch chick movies. *Oh, he drives a rusty pickup?* Too bad, so sad. Time to move on.

3) Showering you with precious gems is always a smart move. But if you need a 100X microscope to see those suckers, cut your losses and hit the road. Big Girls need Big Jewelry, it's in our blood.

4) If he mentions things like stock options, financial portfolios, and his summer house in Nantucket, Big Girl, *you have struck gold.* If he pays for dinner with dirty coins fished from the pocket of his work pants and invites you to share a longneck at the public boat dock, well, really, are you *that desperate?* I hope not, bless your heart!

5) Ex-wives and children are never acceptable, unless his last name is Trump or Gates or Murdock. Hobble away as fast as your swollen ankles will carry you.

6) Are you having difficulty determining the financial solidity of your intended beau? Big Girl, that is why God invented *pay stubs!* Send him out for fried chicken and rummage through those file drawers!

7) The man possesses three homes, a yacht, fourteen cars, and a castle in Spain, but is bald and seventy-two. *WHAT ARE YOU WAITING FOR? HE COULD DROP DEAD ANY SECOND!* Get yourself to the justice of the peace and make it legal, pronto, then call me, so we can spend his money, ok?

My goodness, if one didn't know any better, one might think that this chapter only deals with how to be catty and trick men of wealth and eligibility into marrying us. Pat yourself on the back, Miss Smarty Pants. You got it. For the rest of you unfortunate souls who will be forced to work for a living, please move on to the next chapter.

Chapter Nine

Heaving Yourself Up The Career Ladder

This will be a relatively brief chapter because Big Girls can now, at long last, break the blubber ceiling. Here are my **Big Girl Career Idols:**

1) *Camryn Manheim.* Wrote a great book, *Wake Up, I'm Fat* and set fat chicks free. Won all kinds of awards for her role on TV's *The Practice,* and to top it off, played Snow White, the end-all, be-all feminine Vision of Beauty, in a mini-series. You rock, Camryn!

2) *Oprah.* How can you not love a woman who shares her weight loss secrets, food secrets, and favorite fried chicken recipe with an adoring public, plus she makes no bones about the fact that she battles weight every day of her life, and she fails sometimes! She is human, just like the rest of us, and we thank her for it. We love you, O!

3) *Lainie Kazan.* Recently of *My Big Fat Greek Wedding,* Lainie wrote the Book on Being a Big Girl with Sass and

Class and Attitude, waaaay before it was cool to be a Big Girl. This talented gal does it all, and does it with so much style it makes me weep for joy. Atta girl, Lainie!

4) *Queen Latifah.* If she's not a Class Act, I don't know what is. This girl has spunk, soul, sexy, and saucy down pat. Lordy be, that girl can sing!

5) *Star Jones.* Let 'er rip, honey, all the way to the bank!

6) *Emme.* Not exactly a size 5X, but she's held her own in the Fashion World against twigs, and she certainly fills out a pair of jeans the way God intended!

7) *Kathy Bates.* Any woman over the age of 45 who disrobes in a hot tub with Jack Nicholson, and insists they film it, is one Tough Cookie, ladies! A toast to you, Kathy!

8) *Dolly Parton.* Dolly is on this list because she is one helluva savvy, kick-ass businesswoman, and because she is a Former Big Girl who won her weight battle. I'd have Dolly on my team any ol' day, with guns blazin'!

9) *Nia Vardalos. My Big Fat Greek Wedding* is one of my all-time favorite flicks, right up there with *Muriel's Wedding.* Both movies involve Big Girls Who Win the Guy and Find True Happiness, YAY!

Add to this list Marilyn Monroe, Kathy Najimy, Kathy Kinney, Ricki Lake, Mama Cass, and Aretha Franklin. The list could stretch from here to the taco stand, and it can include *you.* To all Big Girls Everywhere who are told they can never cut the professional mustard until they lose weight, get in shape, or worse, they're never actually talked to, but are repeatedly passed over for a good job, a deserved promotion, or a raise in pay, take a long look at the list above. Most of the women on that list overcame serious odds of all kinds, including their weight, to rise to the top of their respective professions.

As my dad says: *You could if you really wanted to.* He's right. We can truly do anything we want to, it's just that losing weight or getting in shape isn't always the first thing on our to-do list. But every Big Girl on earth has the power to take control of her situation. You can't always do it alone, and you've gotta have a fire in your belly *(how apropos)* that surpasses every objection to your success that you can muster.

So get your Big Girl Attitude in gear, do your research and your homework, buy yourself a *no-holds-barred-I'm-lookin'-gooood* outfit, and lay it on the line, ladies. But please, above all, follow **Big Girl Secret Tip #22:** *If you're in a dead-end professional situation, or in any dead-end situation for that matter, you have only yourself to blame if you stay there. Go back to school, take out a loan, tidy up that resumé or quit your stressful job and work at the hardware store for a few weeks until you can sort it all out. But for heaven's sake, get off your Big Girl Backside and do something positive to change your life! No whining, either! You can if you really want to, and nobody's gonna do it for you, so let's go! And while you're at it, redefine your definition of success. Misery at any level is still misery. Do the thing you love, follow your heart and your dreams, and the money will happen. How do I know this? I followed my dream and now you're reading my book. Thanks for sharing my passion!*

Chapter Ten

Travel, Hobbies & Amusements

Travel is alternatively a gift from the Vacation gods or a visit to the depths of hell, depending upon your ticket class, jet lag quotient, and the availability of snack food in the places you are forced to frequent as a traveler-in-limbo. During the years when I traveled to Europe for business on a regular basis, I frequently heard Big Girl insults aimed at my person in foreign languages. One of the most memorable was with my Big Girl Friend the International Traveler as we journeyed through Germany on my Virgin Business Trip to Europe. I admit, I was a Big Girl moving target ... far too many suitcases, white tennis shoes, and both of us chubsters, which automatically meant we were either from Russia or from the USA. Since our clothing wasn't vintage 1950s, one young man in the train station rightly nailed us as U.S. citizens. He did so by staring us up and down, quite rudely in fact, then said in a loud, sarcastic voice to his gnarly looking friends, the Grungy Guys Who Hang in Train Stations Gang, *"You big girls are looking like Americans, eh?"*

My Big Girl International Traveler Friend, who speaks about ten languages and whom I idolized at that very moment, gave him a tongue-lashing in perfect German that would have made the Nazis seem like pussycats. For the final touch *(TRANSLATION: LAST WORD),* she held her chest high, clutched her Big Girl American Breasts, and said, "Too bad, you ass-wipe, you'll never have the chance to see these babies again!" He was stunned, and my friend never blinked.

I quickly learned that as a Big Girl Who was Raised to Be, Above All Things, *Nice,* I didn't have the fortitude to insult people outside my homeland, although I could hold my own in a couple languages myself. I realized that the easiest way to avoid a Serious Threat to World Peace would be for me to hide my frame underneath a thin raincoat, despite the weather. This worked quite well ... it looked rather chic, coattails flapping wildly in the breeze, it disguised unwanted pounds, and, due to the extreme European popularity of a sci-fi television show, many folks confused me for a Big Girl version of *Highlander. There can be only one Big Girl ... leave me alone or I'll run you through with my loaf of French bread, buster!*

For the most part, though, travel of any sort is no picnic, until you get to your fun destination, so here are a few major **Big Girl Travel Obstacles to Negotiate:**

1) *Seat width.* The old adage is true: there really is more of us to love. When we're forced to pack it all into an airplane, particularly that cunning instrument of Airline Torture,

the Middle Seat, it's a useless situation. Seat width also becomes problematic on trains, buses, at sporting events where the numbers on the bleacher seats practically touch each other, and any place where a cartoon stick figure would be uncomfortable. **My Big Girl Solution:** Write a book/song/movie, become rich and famous, and fly First Class. Or marry well and buy your own plane.

2) *Public bathroom stalls.* This is one of my pet peeves, let me tell you. I am a human being with *needs,* albeit Big Girl ones. In order for me to address those needs, I would prefer to walk into the stall and sit on the toilet without performing a contortionist act that would have put Harry Houdini out of business. Could you bathroom architect people out there *PLEASE* just make the stall doors *SWING OUT?* Is that too much to ask?

3) *Hellish gate changes.* Why is it that you've just arrived at Gate B-32 in Atlanta, you have roughly three minutes to haul your Big Girl frame and your Big Girl Luggage to make a connection, and the Red-Coated Person with the Fake Smile politely informs you that your departure gate is now Z-357. You are required to sprint through the airport *(never a good look for Big Girls, especially when you're trying to eat a sundae),* squeeze onto the underground tram, and shove your way onto an escalator with approximately fourteen square inches of available space. It just ain't gonna happen. If you're a Smart Big Girl, you'll slow down, finish that sundae, and fake a sprained ankle. This shouldn't be a stretch, since your ankles probably swelled on the plane ride anyway. So fake away, and then you can ride that little beeping cart to the ticket counter and re-book your flight in style.

4) *Lost luggage.* Once my suitcase went to Los Angeles, while I traveled to North Carolina. There is an appreciable difference between L.A. and North Carolina, but apparently the luggage handlers didn't think so. Lucky for me I was visiting my Almost-Big Girl Friend and not on a business trip. Lucky for the man at the lost luggage counter that I didn't snap his spine when he offered me a mere $25 to purchase new Big Girl clothes and toiletries. Losing luggage is an Exercise in the Stupidity of the Human Race. For three days, the airline brought an endless stream of suitcases to my Almost-Big Girl Friend's house, imploring me to take one and claim it as my own black garment bag. One van driver even opened up a nice red suitcase and said, *"Look, here's a pair of brand new running shoes. Are you sure these aren't yours?"* Do I *LOOK* like I *RUN*? This was back in the days when procuring Big Girl clothes was no easy task, so it's not like I could just go shopping at one of the thousands of Big Girl Clothing Purveyors available today, although I'm positive, however, that after three days of wearing the same outfit, my Almost-Big Girl Friend was probably ready to shell out some serious cash on my behalf. Finally my suitcase decided its little jaunt to Los Angeles was over, and I got my clothes back. I shouldn't complain, because I have a Traveling Big Girl Friend who once witnessed her suitcase as it bobbed in the ocean, the victim of some kind of horrible sea-plane-luggage transport accident. Can you imagine how difficult it would be to shop for Big Girl business clothes in Japan? *Ahh, so, a size 4,073 …*

5) *Travel with mental patients.* I once found myself in the garden spot that is Myrtle Beach in the middle of summer, on business with a client, who was arguably the skinniest

girl I've ever known next to a Supermodel, but since I don't personally know any Supermodels, why did I just say that? Anyway, this gal had arms like toothpicks and dry toast was her junk food of choice. By the end of the trip, I was ready to snap those toothpick arms in two just to hear her scream. Her idea of a wild evening was to spend serious cash on fake flowers at one of those cheesy "pottery" stores. Then she insisted that she tote home the World's Largest Fruit Basket, given to her by our host. I have nothing against fruit baskets, mind you, but I do resent being forced to act as a pack mule in order to haul this wraith-of-a-girl's produce all the way back to Nashville, via a taxi, an airport shuttle, two planes, and three airports. *Why did I do this,* you ask? Because she was *the client.* Her hands were so full of shopping bags she couldn't see straight, and because she said, *"You're a pretty big girl, here, carry this."* I admit I'm the first kid in the class to take food on a field trip, but you will never, *ever, I swear,* catch me wagging a pile of waxy fruit through an airport *again.*

Well, after that sordid tale, I'm going to have to take a break or my veins will burst through my skin. While I'm riding the Anger Train to Cardiac Arrest, this is probably an excellent time to discuss my **Big Girl Pet Peeves with Respect to Cars:**

1) *Two-door models without a construction crane as a standard feature.* I am fully aware that a sleek sports coupe is not built with Big Girls in mind, but dang it, we look *so good* in one, we just can't stay away. Getting into a hot sports car is usually not the issue, it's getting out. When I owned one of these babies, I frequently sat in the car until

I could flag down someone who looked as though he or she might be a Good Samaritan. It's quite simple to fake a back spasm and ask for help, believe me. See if you can work on this crane thing, Detroit, please.

2) *Steering wheels that don't tilt.* I have two options when entering a car: I can *a)* squeeze my Big Girlness into the seat and immediately drive to the nearest fire station to have the steering wheel surgically removed from my internal organs, or I can *b)* stay home. Most Big Girls purchase cars with the tilt-a-wheel thing included. It's the rental cars you have to watch out for. You think, *I can fit in there, I'll just hop in and adjust the seat,* but after packing yourself into a space that is the equivalent of a gallon-sized freezer bag, you realize that the seat adjustment buttons are near the floor, and not at all visible to you in your present state of physical immobility. I caution you, Big Girls, don't play around with those buttons unseen. I once accidentally pushed a pre-programmed switch and very nearly rammed myself and my new steering wheel appendage through the windshield of a late-model economy car.

3) *Seat belts.* You liberal safety mongers out there may as well put this book down right now and order a pizza, because you're not going to like this one bit. My philosophy on seat belts is that they ruin my Big Girl *Fashionista* style. Since I'm already a distant 4,000th to every other female present at a business meeting or social engagement by virtue of being a Big Girl, I refuse to add unsightly creases to my nicely pressed linen clothing just because a bunch of collision experts spend a bazillion dollars a year cracking up perfectly good automobiles to see if they will break. The

other reason I abhor seat belts *(yes, I realize they could save my life. But if I don't look good in the process ...)* is that I have not yet been introduced to a seat belt that stays where it is supposed to, that is, around my Big Girl mid-section, instead of clinging to my Big Girl neck. Certainly the odds of dying from driving around with a seat belt-obstructed windpipe are much greater than the odds of demise without said seat belt, aren't they? Someone, please do a study, *soon.* This is just my opinion, so don't go out and stop wearing your seat belt. Besides, I'm a *Certified Professional Big Girl Driver on a Closed Course; Do Not Try* unless you work for the collision experts. If you do, stuff a pillow in your shirt next time you go out for a head-on crash and see how it feels to routinely suffer from windpipe burn just by driving to the market.

Whew, did I vent or what? Must be time for something fun-based, so let's move on to Big Girl Hobbies and Amusements. Do you have any favorites? Every Big Girl needs them. To save time, and since I could really use a beer and a sandwich platter, here is my **List of Recommended Hobbies and Amusements for Big Girls:**

1) *Go to the movies.* This is my one true passion, with the exception of ice cream. Where else can you drop a significant amount of cash to see three dozen bad previews, 14 candy commercials, and the latest Cute Hollywood Hunk in living color on the big screen? **Big Girl Secret Tip #23:** *Buy a box of chocolate covered peanuts, dump them in the laundry-tub-sized vat of popcorn you just bought for the bargain price of $25, and munch to your heart's desire. Sharing is a mortal sin.*

2) ***Watch your husband walk the dog.*** What a great way to spend family time together! He and the dog get out of your hair *(oops, I mean bond)* while you sit leisurely on the front porch, thinking about a snack. And speaking of dogs, the bigger the better for us Big Girls, ok? A Saint Bernard at your side is the equivalent of a forty-pound weight loss, the effect is that slimming. Besides, you don't want to risk a Senseless Pet Murder by accidentally stepping on and squashing that little rat-dog you're so fond of, now do you? Get yourself a big dog. You can hear them coming.

3) ***Read*** People *magazine.* It's fun and so cleansing to live vicariously through celebrities, and the articles are intriguing, really. I swear! Plus it's easy to munch on a snack and simultaneously turn the pages.

4) ***Eat at new restaurants.*** This requires no explanation.

5) ***Watch the Food Channel.*** Ditto.

6) ***Power napping.*** Double ditto.

We should at this point review some **Big Girl Hobbies to Avoid At All Costs:**

1) ***Canoeing.*** If I have to explain this to you, you should return to your hometown and repeat high school physics.

2) ***Ballet.*** Sure, they make Big Girl leotards. It's the old boards in the dance floor that scare me.

3) *Tightrope walking or bungee jumping.* Big Girls, gravity is not our friend.

Now we've come to the section in the book where I ask you, Reader Extraordinaire, to pretend you are a well-paid author, living the High Life on a Publicity Tour, and write down in this space those things that you would like to begin as a Hobby, or those activities you, by personal experience and great embarrassment, have learned to avoid. My blood sugar is low, I gotta have a snack.

Chapter Eleven

Parties

As a Single Big Girl, I dreaded parties because I hated to place myself in potentially vile social situations where thousands of Pretty Girls and Handsome Eligible Men made small talk that didn't include me or any of my Big Girl interests, namely Channel Surfing and Power Snacking. There was always the question of What to Wear, When to Arrive, and What to Eat to Avoid Looking Piggy. For many years I would dress for the engagement, drive to said engagement, then sit in my car, too terrified to venture inside. Often I would drive to the nearest restaurant and have dessert, while I invented tales of what the party might be like in order to tell my friends and colleagues the next day. Due to the many social obligations in which my advertising and marketing career often placed me, I had to tough it out and come out of my shell. Thus I quickly developed detailed strategies and tactics for **Successful Party Attendance for Big Girls,** which I will share, out of the goodness of my heart, since you paid big bucks for this book:

Strategies and Tactics for Successful Party Attendance for Big Girls:

1) *Scarlett O'Hara's Mammy was a very clever Big Girl, indeed.* Remember how Mammy made Miss Scarlett eat in her room before sashaying off to the Twelve Oaks barbecue? She knew all eyes would be on Scarlett the Raving Beauty, and that nobody likes to watch another person eat, unless it's chocolate-covered strawberries in the middle of a passion-pit session with your enamored beau, and that is very different. Mammy made Scarlett fill her tiny tummy in advance, so her hands were free from food and therefore free to flirt, most likely because back then Marriageable Men watched you like a hawk to calculate what it would cost to feed a prospective wife. I mean, times were tough on the ol' plantation and you'd much prefer a Girl Who Eats Like a Bird to a Big Girl Who Eats Everything in Sight. Take a tip from Mammy, have a snack of biscuits with sausage and gravy, maybe add a couple of eggs on the side, wash it down with a quart of milk, and you'll be so satisfied you won't even notice the location of the banquet table when you arrive. *Right.*

2) *Wear comfortable shoes at all costs.* You look so ultra-fab in that Big Girl black dress and heels, but *let's review:* after an hour of standing around in one place making small talk, or eavesdropping on everyone else's, your ankles are going to become the size of New Hampshire. *This is not a good look for you,* Big Girl. Save those heels for funerals and toss on your cross-trainers, because otherwise you're in for severe edema and a mid-party trip to the ER. Everyone on the streets of New York wears running shoes with dress clothes

all the time, and no one bats an eye. Look at Cybill Shepherd. She's a glamorous Tall Girl and she wears nothing but tennies with her designer outfits. She practically double-dog dares anybody to tell her not to. You *go, Cybill!* Make a statement!

3) ***Tiaras are not an appropriate Big Girl party accessory.*** I realize that when you were seven, you were as thin as a rail and you won the Little Miss Pumpkin Patch Beauty Pageant. But wearing a tiara on your Big Girl head in hopes that a gentleman partygoer will inquire about it, so you can relay to him the fact that you have not always been this size, is not a good idea. Better to snag a photo of your svelte sister, whip it out and say, *"Yes, before I put on a few pounds to land that role in a major motion picture, this was me. According to my trainer, it's only a matter of weeks before that Thin Princess returns!"* If he does not immediately ask for your phone number, he is obviously damaged goods and you should move on anyway.

4) ***Never arrive on time.*** You already face increased scrutiny as a Big Girl, so don't add to your stress level by arriving early when you're sure to stick out like a sore thumb. Wait a minute ... there isn't anything thumb-like about Big Girls, maybe it should be *stick out like a sore Longhorn steer.* Anyway, my recommendation is if the party begins at seven, arrive at eight. The crowd will be thick as hornets and this allows you to blend, if that is possible. Large plants are excellent vantage points for blending, by the way, and you can use the planter as a drink stand.

5) ***Head straight for the adult beverages.*** This is fairly self-

explanatory, but the point here is that you will release your Inner Big Girl Party Spirit after a couple of stiff drinks or an entire bottle of wine. Not only will you amaze everyone with your jolly laughter and raucous wit, you'll be oblivious to insults or nasty comments made in your vicinity. If things get out of hand, you can pass out and fall to the floor in a Drunken Big Girl Heap. But be forewarned, if this happens, nobody's likely to offer to hoist you into a spare bedroom, so you may have to spend the night prone on the exquisite tile in the foyer or out in the yard by the pool house. That's why you should always wear black, to avoid mud stains. *Trust me on this.*

6) *Never lean against furniture or sit on the arms of chairs, particularly antiques.* Less statuesque humanoids have frequent opportunities to look *trés chic* at parties by casually leaning against an armoire or sitting lightly on the arm of a chair while balancing a plate of food. *DO NOT ATTEMPT THIS, <u>EVER</u>!* The furniture may slide out from under your Big Girl person and out the window, or the arm of the chair might break right off and a chicken wing from your plate could smack you in the face. This is Certain Future Party Invitation Death. Avoid it at all costs!

7) *Latch on to a geeky guy.* This on-the-ball action is sure to prevent the Big Girl from standing solo all evening. Hey, I'm not saying you have to bear this man's children. Just hang with him for the better part of the evening. Believe me, most Geeks would give their horn-rimmed glasses to have any type of female companionship at their side during a party, laughing at their Geeky Rocket Scientist jokes.

He'll thank you for it. You might snag a dinner date on the side, and he may be rich …

8) *Find the kitchen.* A Smart Big Girl Party-Goer has satisfied her appetite at home, in private, pre-party. But it's now around midnight, things are starting to break up, and to say you're hungry is to say that SARS is the equivalent of a slight head cold. If you know the location of the kitchen, you can make a beeline in search of free nutritional sustenance, most likely in private, because the other guests have probably paired off and are necking in the woods or the hot tub by now. Skip the *hors d'oeuvres,* they've been sitting out for at least five hours and there's this revolting bacteria known as *salmonella* that can do a number on a Big Girl's intestinal tract. Head straight for the extra dessert tray. Do the hostess a favor, she would be ashamed to know that those chocolate truffles and *petit fours* she was so proud of were hardly touched. It is your duty as a Big Girl to be a good guest and eat the remaining desserts, *natch!*

9) *Stake out your own Big Girl territory.* In my personal annals of party-going experience, this rarely happens, but *let's review* to be prepared. If the unthinkable occurs and you are not the only Big Girl at the soirée, by all means don't hang with your competition, or the other guests might think:
   a) *You're a couple*
   b) *There's an impromptu weight loss meeting in the living room*
   c) *Isn't that sweet, she brought her twin sister*
   d) *Those lazy caterers are just standing around talking and not doing their job*

Defend your Big Girl territory at all costs, do whatever it takes, and make sure you beat your competition to the Kitchen *(#8, above)* or you'll be stuck with the bacteria-laden, five-hour-old cheese dip for sustenance.

10) *Never claim lost party undergarments.* **A Case in Point:** Once I was privileged to attend a very wild, exceedingly drunken bash at the home of a colleague. In the confusion, and believe me, it was very confusing trying to make my legs work the way God intended and carry my lard ass out to the car, my slip fell off. The following day, my colleague politely brought said undergarment to the national sales meeting, held it aloft, and announced, *"Does this belong to anyone?"* Do you think I have mush for brains? No way was I going to admit that this piece of ratty polyester resembling the mainsail on a frigate belonged to me. I cleverly deflected curious onlookers by confidently stating, *"Don't look at me. I was wearing slacks!"* and of course they were all so hungover they couldn't think straight, so I was spared Horrible Big Girl Undergarment Embarrassment.

Congratulations, you have now learned the **Strategies and Tactics for Successful Party Attendance for Big Girls,** and you have my permission to put yourself out into society. There is only one reason you should refrain from meeting your social obligations, and that is if you have in your possession a half-gallon of Rocky Road ice cream and a bag of Oreos. Much better to stay home with your real friends and channel surf ...

Chapter Twelve

As Seen On TV

One of my favorite things to do on a rainy, winter Saturday is turn on the boob tube and watch infomercials in varying degrees of hilarity and believability. If I'm really motivated, I'll remove the drip-drying panty hose and other laundry items from my treadmill, turn it on, and slowly walk as I watch, wearing my Frumpy At-Home Outfit *(see Chapter Six, Clothes, Makeup, Hair & Its Removal)*. A serious fitness buff would dust off the Stair-stepper, open the box to the Ab-o-Matic, break-out the unused Cardio-Slide, or as a last resort, remove the Thigh Murderer from its place of honor in my office, where it's been used as a doorstop since 1991. But you're near the end of this book, and you have certainly figured out by now I'm anything but a fitness buff. I prefer to exercise vicariously through models on TV, in the comfort of my own home, where the supply of cookies never ends. Here is **Big Girl Secret Tip #24:** *Before tuning the television to an infomercial or home shopping* *program, visit your neighborhood lobotomist to have your credit card numbers electrically removed from your brain stem. Cutting up the cards doesn't work. I know this for a fact, so get drastic and be prepared.*

Early Saturday mornings are Infomercial Heaven for Bad TV junkies like me. With new batteries in the remote and a steaming cup of hot chocolate at my side, I'm rarin' to go. The first selection of the day is one of my personal favorites, Richard Simmons. This is great fun to watch, and Richard makes us Big Girls feel understood and good about ourselves, despite the fact that we can't leave the house through the door. Any diet plan that combines food with poker, count me right in. Let's be honest, Big Girls out there … haven't you always dreamed that Richard Simmons would come to your house, hug you on the neck, and listen in earnest, tears streaming down his face, as you tell your Weight Loss Success Story? Richard, you're amazing. Keep up the good work. But you might tone it down a bit, buddy. No one can be that incessantly perky without the aid of amphetamines. You're scaring me, ok? I worry about you.

Flip to Billy Blanks and his exercise system. Now at the outset, Billy seems to have his stuff together. This infomercial has excellent production value, which means that the Size Two beauties in Lycra sports bras and hot pants get to hop around looking cute and sipping mineral water while Billy talks about his life-changing fitness experiences and how they can work for *you.* This form of exercise is no doubt fulfilling and results-oriented, plus you get to kick and punch the hell out of anything you can imagine that aggravates you, like your boss, your ex-husband, or the dress you can't fit into that you'd planned to wear to a fancy party tonight. But Billy, I gotta tell you, take a tip from your pal Richard, there, and get some *FAT CHICKS* on the set. I want to see how long they last without oxygen or a trip to the emergency room.

Next on the agenda are an ex-Supermodel and a former Texas Ranger promoting their particular instrument of exercise torture. As a former Texan, I'd do just about anything for a certified Texas Ranger, or a guy who played one on TV. This man could read the phone book and I'd probably sign over my entire estate, in short order. But the supermodel connection confuses me … supermodels don't eat, so how can they have a weight problem? *Go figure.*

The machine they promote looks like an excellent way to tone up and lose weight, but I can't get past how narrow that bench is. I mean, how in the heck is my Big Girl Butt supposed to stay put while I do all those exercises? My derrière would no doubt extend over the edges by at least two inches on each side *(another reason the phrase "let's go bicycling" never escapes my lips).* I'm thinking this is probably not right for me.

Flip the channel … NO! It's *The All-Natural, Green, Rip-off-the-Skin-with-your-Hair Gel people! CHANGE! CHANGE!* Whew, that was a close call. All those horrid memories of that particular hair removal disaster came flooding back. I thought I was gonna need to call the Skin Graft Center Hotline for a second. Flip, flip … a show about All-Natural Nutritional Supplements … the one they fed to obese mice, and the mice subsequently lost all their body mass, including their skin, bones, and virtually any trace of their existence. *Naah,* the only natural supplement this Big Girl needs is chocolate. Flip, flip, flip …

Oh, this one's been around for a while. It's Suzanne Somers and her various and sundry "master" machines. Sorry, Suzanne. I hate to disappoint you, but Big Girls would need a Whole Body Master, although I guess a thigh or a butt would be a start in the right direction. You are in good shape, girl. You rock!

Flip, flip ... it's a ponytailed guy on a machine that looks like it could launch me across the room and do serious bodily damage to my internal organs. This is in the same exercise equipment family as the product featuring enormous rubber bands. You are supposed to tie yourself up, then attempt to walk to the closest convenience store against the resistance. My luck, I'd reach out to take a step, the rubber band would break, and I'd be out cold and get run over in my own driveway. I really don't think so ... hospital food *sucks!*

Flip, flip ... ah, here's something I can sink my teeth into ... the Food Channel. Today's special program is "Cooking Enough to Satisfy Fat People." Man, are these folks on my wavelength, or what?

Chapter Thirteen

Spirituality & Meditation

If anything positive can be said about me, in addition to being a Jolly Big Girl, it's that I have a strong faith in God. I know for a fact that God does exist: I only need to look at the face of my son and *WHAM,* all doubts disappear. I've had some extremely close calls or extraordinary experiences that all seem to point to that 9-1-1 Center in the Sky. I'm thankful for those life-examining moments, as well as the aid given.

Perhaps due to my unique perspective as a Big Girl and a Believer, I am often baffled at the way people treat one another. I'm not one to preach or harangue folks about their individual spiritual practices, so here is **Big Girl Secret Tip #25:** *Let's all just play nice and get along. It's a big planet, and for the most part we're intelligent. So let's stop killing each other and whining about who has the best nuclear bombs or the most oil, and just share, ok?*

As a student of things mystical and mysterious, which is a source of great concern to my ultra-Lutheran family, I practice my faith and yet possess great respect for all the world's religions and what they have to offer in terms of peaceful messages and the care of our Earth and one another. Although I recognize that yoga is a powerful tool to seek one's inner sanctum and reflect on your Big Girl Oneness with the Universe, it is virtually physically impossible for me and many other Big Girls to practice yoga without sustaining serious and permanent bodily injury.

Thus I developed my own form of meditational exercise, exclusively for Big Girls. It is entitled *Hurt Me Until I Confess.* I must be brief in this section, because I'm pretty sure there are a few spies from the Vatican lurking in my front yard, in an effort to seize this new program and use it to their financial gain.

Let's review the basic tenets of *Hurt Me Until I Confess,* shall we?

1) It's my way, or the highway. If you're so smart, dream up your own meditational exercise program. You cannot steal components of my routine and enhance them with items used by the Baptists, infamous for curricula including *Give Until It Hurts, Fire and Brimstone Jumping 101,* and *Wave Your Arms Above Your Head for Three Hours Straight.* Neither will I accept the legendary tactic developed by the Lutherans, *Guilt As a Load-Bearing Exercise.* There is absolutely no place in this program for serpents of any kind, including televangelists.

2) I'm fully aware of *"the body is a temple"* principle, so I don't

want to hear one word about why I can't grasp the concept of permanent weight loss. Perhaps I have an extra-large soul that requires an extra-large temple. Besides, who the hell are you to judge, anyway?

3) Meditation should take about a minute and a half in your office chair, tops. Otherwise your legs lose all circulation and you have to spend the rest of the afternoon hoisting yourself around with your hands, which is never a good career move, and often impossible for a Big Girl. I, the instructor, am the only one authorized to stop meditating, for any reason whatsoever as I see fit, including the nourishment of my Big Girl self with a snack. If you can't deal with this, twist yourself into a pretzel and give your tantric yoga buddy Sting a call, ok?

Now that we've established the *Hurt Me Until I Confess* ground rules for clearing our heads and baring our souls, please follow along closely or I shall be forced to smack you on the forehead with my PDA. **Here are the basic positions for the no-fail, spiritual oneness-attaining meditational exercise,** *Hurt Me Until I Confess:*

1) Sit in any wheeled office chair with your back straight, arms relaxed, and your feet in front of you approximately 24 inches away from your desk.

2) Extend your arms at your sides, inhaling deeply, then raise them to the ceiling. Release your tension, release all your thoughts of worldly possessions, and your goal to dominate world commerce. Let go of your transgressions, including the Mortal Sin wherein you ate all your son's

leftover Easter candy after you told him it had expired and would prove fatal if he touched it. Now exhale, and bring your arms back to a resting position.

3) Take your left foot, hook it slightly behind the back-most roller on your chair and *STRETCH*. Good! Lean into it. *Excellent*. Now keep your left foot where it is. Bring your arms behind your back and lock your hands behind you … *slowly, slowly,* very nice. Now repeat the left foot pattern with your right foot, making certain to *BREATHE*. Very good. Have you tried this type of exercise before? You will soon be a master, young Padewan!

4) Expel all your inner demons into the universe with several deep, cleansing breaths.

5) Now, this is the most critical part and must be done correctly to achieve *Total Meditational Cleansing* … lean forward until you fall over, flat on your face *(but please try to avoid hitting the desk)*. This will require some practice, so don't be a wimp and quit. It is imperative to enlist the aid of an assistant whose job is to remove the office chair from your backside, otherwise serious damage to the chair may occur. Then, God help us, the lawyers will come out of the woodwork.

6) *BAM!* You should be down for a full count of twenty. When you awaken, you will feel utterly refreshed and ready to take on the world. All those negative feelings toward mankind will have vanished, as well as your name and cell phone number. But that's why God invented the *My Cell Phone* screen, to aid you on your personal faith journey!

Now then, isn't that easy? Don't you feel *GREAT?* This Meditational Exercise is not solely limited to Big Girls … anyone can do it with the right motivation and a little desire. And fear not, ye Skeptical Big Girls, if **Hurt Me Until I Confess** isn't your bag. No sweat! Spirituality is a very personal journey. Just get some and spread it around, ok?

Conclusion

Congratulations! You have completed your intense, personal examination of *The Big Girls' Guide to Life,* and should now fully possess the requisite tools to aid you on your journey to Ultimate Happiness and Fulfillment. *Right.* Yeah, look at it this way: You probably enjoyed a couple of laughs at the expense of others, namely, *moi,* and if that isn't worth the purchase price, I'll be damned what is.

Remember, Big Girls, that your life is what you make it. You Have the Power to eat the entire bag of Oreos and drink a half-gallon of skim milk while you watch Oprah, or skip Oprah altogether and do sit-ups for an hour. It's your choice. I have tried, in my best I-am-not-a-medical-expert-nor-do-I-play-one-on-TV manner, to provide you with the information you need to bring a healthy balance to your world; to allow you to free your soul and express your inner beauty; and to love your neighbor as yourself, with the sole exception of sharing your last piece of fudge.

Whatever you do, Big Girl, keep a smile on that pretty face *(it's such a pretty face, isn't it?),* and remember that being a Big Girl, although she wasn't as big as some, worked for Bridget Jones. She got the guy in the end, and he liked her just the way she was. The key to Big Girl Success in Life is loving yourself so you can be free to love others. If you don't love yourself, cart your hind-end to the bookstore and spend a few hours in the self-help section. For God's sake, it's not rocket science! You may never be a size two, but you can embrace who you are and try to figure out what it is you want in this world. Then get off your duff and go for it, whether it's a hot fudge sundae or a six-pack of abs.

As for me, gentle reader, I will no doubt continue on my journey down the Big Girl Highway, spreading love and lard wherever I go, acting as Mentor and Guide to those hollow-eyed, super-fit yet superficial folks who refuse to treat Big Girls with kindness and respect.

But for now, kids, I'm about to die of *starvation.* This has been a helluva lot of work, so I'm gonna sign off now and go find me a big chicken-fried steak, ok?

About the Author

Bunkie Lynn was born in Tucson, Arizona, raised in the American South, earned a B.S. in Radio-TV-Film from the University of Texas at Austin and now resides near Nashville, Tennessee with her family. A Big Girl herself, Bunkie became a serious writer after forays in advertising, marketing, and international business management. She is a critically acclaimed humorist and speaker, and is currently at work on her next comedic fiction novel, unless a Big Truckload of Money falls from the sky, and then she'll retire to the islands. You may e-mail her at Bunkie@bunkielynn.com.

About C.J. Bach

C.J. has been fighting the battle of the bulge all of her life, and is the proud owner of several closetsful of clothes ranging in size from 14 to 22. She has traveled to more than 70 countries around the globe, and hasn't found many foods she doesn't like! A polyglot, C.J. can say "I'm so FAT!" in 7 different languages (with feeling). C.J. is proud to say that she has completed several half-marathons and a full marathon in the last few years, to the amazement of the less-than-statuesque running community at large!

About the Designer

Klair Kimmey has been in the Graphic Design business in the Knoxville, Tennessee area for almost twenty years. She enjoys it almost as much as spending time with her brilliant (they all say that, but really he is) son and loving husband. You can reach her at kkimmey@earthlink.net.

About the Artist

Rick Baldwin is an award-winning cartoonist and illustrator from Knoxville, Tennessee. His comic strips "Outta Toon" and "All The World" have been published nationally since 1987.

Also by Bunkie Lynn...

A Comedy of Heirs

An elderly woman's fantastical tale of stolen inheritance and murder wreaks havoc with Tennessee debutantes, philanderers, and rednecks as they prepare for the Sons of Glory Festival to honor their Confederate dead. A Comedy of Heirs is a wild, hilarious ride, full of the American South's lingo, raucous characters, and the River Jordan Drive-Thru Car Wash and Baptism. Bunkie Lynn's sarcastic humor has been compared to that of Dave Barry and John Kennedy Toole. (ISBN 0-9721301-0-1)

New in 2004 ...
A Dark Cajun ~~Roux~~ Ruse

In a tiny Cajun Louisiana parish, the mayor has a problem ... his nationally registered Acadian Cemetery is out of plots, and the old folks are dropping like flies. The town's 1756 charter guarantees burial in the beautiful cemetery to every Cajun citizen who dies within city limits, and miraculously, the mayor makes it happen. When a young federal inspector from Maine discovers questionable burial practices within the cemetery, he knows that uncovering a scandal could rocket him up the career ladder, but his priorities change after an enchanting, dark-haired Cajun girl teaches him the Cajun motto, "Laissez les bon temps rouler." This hilarious adventure is a celebration of Cajun culture you'll never forget. (ISBN 0-9721301-2-8)

For author appearance information, visit
www.bunkielynn.com